Anything
Will Be Easy
after This

American Lives | SERIES EDITOR: Tobias Wolff

Anything Will Be Easy after This

A Western Identity Crisis

BETHANY MAILE

University of Nebraska Press | Lincoln

Library of Congress Cataloging-in-Publication Data
Names: Maile, Bethany, author.
Title: Anything Will Be Easy after This: A Western Identity Crisis / Bethany Maile.
Description: Lincoln: University of Nebraska Press, [2020] | Series: American Lives
Identifiers: LCCN 2019041518
ISBN 9781496220219 (paperback)
ISBN 9781496222428 (epub)
ISBN 9781496222435 (mobi)
ISBN 9781496222442 (pdf)
Subjects: LCSH: Maile, Bethany. | West (U.S.)—Description and travel. | West (U.S.)—Social life and customs. | Idaho—Biography.
Classification: LCC F595.3 .M35 2020 | DDC 978—dc23
LC record available at
https://lccn.loc.gov/2019041518

Set in Scala by Laura Buis.

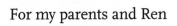

For my parents and Ren

We tell ourselves stories in order to live.

—*Joan Didion*

If we do not evolve, we die.

—*William Kittredge*

Contents

Acknowledgments

This book would not have happened without the support, guidance, and example of a few exceptional writers. I'd like to first thank Ander Monson, whose belief in the early drafts of this project never stopped propelling it forward. I would also like to thank him for teaching me to be playful on the page and for telling me to write like a motherfucker. He said it before it was on a mug, I swear. I am indebted to Aurelie Sheehan, Alison Hawthorne Deming, and Fenton Johnson for their keen insights into the early pages of this book. Without Joy Passanante, Mary Clearman Blew, and Brandon Schrand, I would not have found my way to nonfiction, and I would not have understood the West as an idea that deserves (if not demands) exploration and interrogation. Thank you, Joe Wilkins, Alicia Christensen, and Abigail Stryker for carrying this book into the world.

I have benefited from a dear cohort of friends, readers, and general badasses. Craig Reinbold, Annie Lampman, Margaret Kimball, and Katherine Standefer, for reading the drafts, answering the emails, taking the calls, and being wonderful humans. I owe them many beers.

My friends and family have been my most steadfast believers. Becky MacDonald listened and encouraged and gave me room to write about her life. Tucker Maile's early and fervent support was unmatched. They were my first fans, and I am lucky to have them both. Margo and Jim Hunter, for giving me a room of my own, I am so appreciative. Stacy Haynes, Hallie Vinson, Lewis Drey, Chelsea Klikunas, Ella MacDonald, Daniela Maile, and the other folks who spent time loving my kids so I could wrap up this work, they are godsends, all.

To Ryan I owe more than I can say, so I will leave it at this: what luck, to have him in my corner. And to our daughters, who are the best possible motivation and inspiration, I am grateful for and to them every day.

Finally, I reserve my deepest gratitude for my parents, Tom and Colleen. Thank you for always reminding me that the answer is to just keep going and for helping me—in all of the ways—to do just that. Thank you for keeping books in my lap and a pen in my hand. Thank you for imagining that home on a hill, that pasture of mares bowed and grazing. Thank you for giving me stories to tell.

I wish to thank the following publications for their support of my work:

"Ladies' Night at the Shooting Range," *Prairie Schooner* (2011)
"The Wild Ones," *River Teeth* (2011)
"*True Grit, Country Strong,* and Other Lies: A Taxonomy of Western Women," *Normal School* (2012)
"Anything Will Be Easy after This," *Normal School* (2013)
"The Slaughterhouse," *High Desert Journal* (2017)
"How Lady Antebellum Wrecked Country Music (in Nine Movements)," *Terminus Magazine* (2018)

Anything
Will Be Easy
after This

Going West

The commands were familiar: *Tray tables, seat belts, emergency exits, oxygen masks; save yourself first.* I didn't pay attention. It was 5:30 a.m., and I had a long day ahead: Boston to Chicago, Chicago to Salt Lake, a four-hour layover, and then, finally, Salt Lake to Boise, Idaho. It would be dark. The Treasure Valley would be a constellation of city lights, all of Ada County the Little Dipper. Outside the window Boston was a crosshatching of harbor lights, streetlights, headlights, flashing billboards, a skyscraper lit to read GO SOX. The Big Dipper, Hydra, the Milky Way.

The plane leveled out, takeoff over. Tray tables lowered; seats reclined. I pulled out a copy of Ginsberg's collected works. *He's the shit*, a boy in my literature class had told me. *Keep it.* "Howl" was the only thing I recognized.

> In dreams you walk dripping from a sea-journey on the
> highway
> Across America in tears to the door of my cottage in the
> Western night.

A western cottage. My parents' home: their wrap-around porch and horse pasture; the alfalfa fields that fringed Eagle, Idaho; the broad face of the Boise Mountains; the blue basins of the Owyhees. A dream. I envisioned that wide prairie sky, nothing like the slivers between Back Bay skyscrapers. I pictured my mare bucking at low thunder. I saw Clint Eastwood pull a six-gun; I heard Loretta Lynn's trembled, jingling voice. I smelled spring thaw and wet hay. I barreled toward the Wild West—an illusion, a myth—on a journey with no destination.

Eagle, Idaho, is a farm town–turned–glitzy suburb six miles northwest of the capital city. It is home to the "World's Largest Rocky Mountain Oyster [testicle] Feed," a scatter of farm fields, three bakeries (one irksomely self-described as a "cupcakery"), two golf courses, a town gazebo, a Hilton, and one spa where tiny, forceful women massage rose petals into guests' backs. It is home to a few ranchers and farmers and twenty thousand suburbanites.

Like so many eighteen-year-olds from barely known corners of the country,[1] I was itching to leave, to swap the gravel roads for subway tracks, the hayfield keggers for neon-lit bars, the tract homes for brownstones. After high school I backpacked Europe (which was typical, just another kid scrimping money for train tickets and museum fees) and then enrolled at Emerson College in Boston. Air damp and salty, museums you could get lost in, a fine arts college full of young people who developed Kodak film and pinned French New Wave posters to their walls—all the things I'd felt lacking in Idaho. I went east expecting prep school kids and crew on the Charles River. *School Ties* and *Good Will Hunting*. With those movie-induced expectations, I didn't last a year.

Mary Clearman Blew said, "Stories are a way of explaining the inexplicable, of giving shape to that which has no shape, meaning to that which eludes meaning." There's something to this idea that narrative fills voids. Think of creation stories (how the earth formed off a turtle's back, how woman grew from a rib); they tell us where we are, how we got here, who we've become.

In Idaho's history there is an apt example of this kind of meaning making. When the first white travelers explored the American

West, they were overwhelmed by the vastness, by the perceived emptiness, by all that, as Blew said, eluded meaning. In an attempt to fill this imagined vacancy,[2] they told stories. Fictions that turned to mythologies that haunt this place and its people still.

So people tell stories, in general, as a means of explaining and understanding, but they tell stories about place, in particular, because the relationship between place and person is essential. The sociological theory of place identity says we are all by-products of place, the region that grew us a kind of lineage or heritage or a strand of DNA we carry within us. Place is a means of self-realization, self-actualization.

No one was as surprised by my Boston return as I was. I'd covered sixteen European countries and lived in the Hungarian country-side and had hardly thought of home. If someone had told me I wouldn't even round out a year in Boston, I'd have called bullshit.

I may have implied that my jones for the western myth started in that plane seat, the Boston Bay shrinking below, Loretta Lynn's voice jangling. But dial back a few months. The apartment in Boston sat belowground, and the only good light was in the kitchen. I'd sit on the floor, back against the oven, and flip through the *New York Times*. One morning nothing of note, until this: a picture of a home the color of cattails camped low in a meadow. The Rocky Mountains, jagged and endless, jutted up from a field of sage and cheatgrass. Hills yellowed in the warm light of a waning sun. Split rail fencing—like oversized strings of barbed wire—circled the yard. A meadow electric-yellow with wild mustard seeds. It was Idaho at its most idyllic, a real stunner.

It wasn't just that this picture was familiar—a snippet of home three thousand miles away; it was that it was a picture of Idaho at its most enchanting. The house was dwarfed in the saddle of the valley. There wasn't a single person in sight, and any evidence of civilization (telephone poles, paved roads) had been carefully cropped out. Just mountains, thirteen acres of fenced meadow, and that single home, mine if I wanted it, the picture suggested. In the ad one of the most familiar incarnations of the American dream beat on—*go west, claim land, watch the deer wander and the hawks dive.* It was the familiar story of western possibility, escape, solitude. And I tore it out and stuck it to my fridge.

Thirty years before I boarded that plane home, a swell of young people migrated west. In the 1970s Back-to-the-Landers wanted hand-shucked corn and fresh butter. They bolted from the city and took to the hills. All the hippies were doing it.

In Denver, Colorado, my parents (two such hippies) met and six weeks later married. My father, who had grown up in the rolling mountains of Upstate New York, came to Colorado for law school and fly-fishing and the jutting red teeth of Pikes Peak. In my parents' hutch is a photo of him then: he wears tiny jean cutoffs, a long beard, and wild, waving hair. His head thrown back, he is, I can tell, laughing his full rolling laugh.

My mother said he married her not because she wore red halter tops and snug jeans or because her hair fell in a thick honey mane or because she started college at sixteen but because she made him laugh. That commitment to a good time defined his fatherhood. He was the dad who gave our friends nicknames. Who snuck candy into midnight movies. Who rafted rivers and hiked mountains and rode horses. Who never hesitated when balancing us bareback or guiding us through flashing rapids. He wanted his children sure and steady in the potentially perilous. And when the horse bucked or the raft flipped, when we were stunned or scared, he held our elbow and said tenderly but with clear direction, "Come on now." Adventure, resilience—my father so naturally embodies that western spirit.

In him my mother saw a sort of escape. The only child of a bitter married couple, she had endured a lonely upbringing in the damp gray of Duluth, Minnesota. She lived in a quiet home with plastic liners on the furniture where everything smelled of bleach and wood polish and her mother's Camel cigarettes. With an IQ that launched above the Mensa line, she taught herself to read at age three, and her razor wit sped through conversations. Other kids, I suspect, did not understand her. So she turned to books and the woods for comfort. By the time she finished graduate school, when a cousin invited her to Denver, she busted right out.

Eighteen days after my mother landed in Colorado, she met my father. They lived in the same apartment building—had both chosen it, in fact, for its distance from downtown and its mountain views. They met at a St. Patrick's Day party, where they clinked green beers and danced to Willie Nelson. A week later, when my father's apartment flooded, he banged on her door. My mother opened it and found him in cowboy boots, those little denim cutoffs (so short the pockets hung below the hem), and nothing else. A German shorthair puppy curled in his arm and a fifty-pound bag of dog food balanced on his shoulder.

"I can't have the dog," he said. "Hide him?"

She took the puppy, and he dumped the food in her closet and called the super.

His television, the most expensive thing he owned, was ruined. In the evenings he watched *Mary Hartman* at her place, and to pay his debt, he cooked her liver and onions or lamb chops with mint jelly. They ate on the couch, and the dog slept in her lap. She hadn't landed a job, and she didn't know many people. Twice her friends had flown out to try to lure her back home. But my father looked like Ryan O'Neal. He could break a wild horse and shoot a target dead-on. He was someone who saved the dog's food but left the TV.

They hardly knew each other, but they knew they each imagined a yellow house with a wraparound porch and a full maple out front; a pasture of mares, coats slick after a hard ride; a red barn; a farmhouse on a mini-farm. And this was, essentially, the home they would make. My father would build that house. My mother would plant that maple. They would buy horses and set them to graze that field. Their three kids would jump from the barn's loft and swim in the irrigation ditches. They dreamed a future, and then they built it.

But first they wed in a Rocky Mountain state park. My mother wore a sunbonnet over thick, blonde curls and sewed her dress from eyelet curtains. Guests cleaned chicken thighs with their teeth. My father walked down the aisle with a beer in hand. It was a chill, country affair. For the next year they lived in their Volkswagen Beetle with a couple sleeping bags, that German shorthair named Zeb, and a tent. They circled the West, looking for a place to claim.

They wandered New Mexico, Utah, Arizona, Wyoming. They camped in Yellowstone—its horizon blotted with buffalo herds, its geysers sulfuring the air—and crossed into Idaho. The Wyoming border is a serious knockout—Jackson Hole and the Grand Tetons. But heading west, deeper into Idaho, the scene dries up. The Snake River plain spreads in buttes and clay-colored canyons and tumbleweed and sage. Sun-blasted and eye-wincingly bright. If a traveler keeps plugging west, she will eventually hit Boise.

Idaho is shaped like a boot: fat between Oregon and Wyoming, slim between Washington and Montana, and the Treasure Valley (which is home to Boise) sits just below this northward tapering. It's a gateway, then, to the forested panhandle on the Canada end and the desert plains toward Nevada and Utah. On the north lip of the valley, in a city patriotically named Eagle, my parents' Beetle broke down on a piece of for-sale property, ten acres at the base of the Boise range. Destiny, they've always said.

The West found me in the East. Across from the Coolidge Corner T-stop, thirty minutes from Boston Common, sits Brookline Booksmith, an independent bookshop with deep armchairs and a basement mazed in paperbacks. This is how Mary Clearman Blew came to me. I was not in a regional nonfiction section (if they even had such a thing). I was not hunting for relics of home. But there on the shelf, the spine of *Bone Deep in Landscape*. On the cover a herd of horses stood at attention beneath that familiar, wide sky. I turned the book and read about a fifth-generation Montana rancher who rounded up cattle and hauled water and, I imagined, never didn't have calluses.

Brookline is the place I had expected to love. As a girl, I imagined myself grown and living in a place just like Coolidge Corner—an art deco theater showing independent films; a record shop where cashiers with wrist tattoos knew just the album you were looking for; a park where stay-at-home fathers pushed children on swings. A town square with a bagel shop, an ice cream shop, a bookshop—not a strip mall with *stores*. It was the backdrop to my childhood anticipation. But I rode the train out of Boston, back to the hydrangea-lined stoops of Brookline, and stopped at the bookstore. I paid the cashier and slid Blew's book, with its dappled plains and expectant mares, into my bag.

I remember two things about my last day in Boston. The Common, between the Park Street T-stop and Emerson's campus, was crowded with strollers and joggers and men in suits and younger men with open guitar cases and women with briefcases and twenty-somethings with iPods thumping in their ears, the air sweet with brewed coffee and wet wool, the ground slick with wet leaves. The city pulsed. The sky was bright, the same clear blue as a cold, high desert morning, but there was just one thin angle of it. I remember that slice of sky and buying my plane ticket home.

That day of travel felt like the long wait outside a principal's office, palms hot, gut pitching with dread. My parents were understanding folks. When I said I'd wanted to study writing, my father spent two weeks driving me around New England, touring campuses. My mother bought me books with titles like *Nail Your Novel* and *Unlocking the Writing Within*. Never pressure. Just support. But this felt like I'd been caught exchanging a Christmas sweater. I felt ungrateful. After six months in an expensive apartment in an expensive city studying the arts at an expensive college, one day I had just hopped a plane home.

For all my parents' kindness the months I spent "regrouping" (as my mother gently put it) were lacquered in late-teen angst. Think *Garden State* or *The Graduate*—the young adult returned, dazed, stuck. I slept in my old bunk bed and got a part-time job at the Gap. Over the lunch break I ate corn dogs in the food court. After a shift, a couple of dollar movies. Chilling at the mall and movieplex, like I was sixteen again. Depressing as hell.

But this is a story about myths, about meaning making, about using narrative to understand place and by association ourselves. In 1859 the government sent Albert Bierstadt west to capture, as he called it, "that wild region." He sent back paintings of ultra-dramatic landscapes: light tints mountains in gold, storm clouds pregnant with rain shade meadows and turn the whole scene fecund. Dramatic to the max, Romantic in the deepest sense.

Romance becomes another word for *fiction, illusion, myth*. But the word feels even more loaded. Romance is mythic in that it has "no foundation in fact," but it's also the "belief in something fabulous" (so says the *Oxford English Dictionary*). So romance combines the extraordinary with factlessness. It puts faith in the best version of a story, and this combination (how alluring this impossible dream) is what keeps people suckered.

But to say I bailed on college and ran lickety-split home just because I felt romantic might be an overstatement. A lot of things were at play: a boyfriend I'd left behind, the unforgivable cost of a liberal arts education, and—maybe most potently—that dream of steaming meadows, frost smoking beneath the heat of a just-risen sun. But I knew better, had spent my whole life in the prairies and cul-de-sacs outside Boise, Idaho. There were more malls than mercantiles, more minivans than pickup trucks. This story was more fiction than fact. But knowing all that, I dreamed just the same.

This weakness to romance is essential to the western identity. Three years after Bierstadt's trek, the Homestead Act famously promised 160 acres to any white man who could "improve the land," which usually meant figuring out a way to water their lot—no small task. The government hadn't advertised that most of the West was tough-to-farm desert, and to make matters worse, the land was nearly lumberless (as most deserts are), so farmers had no way to fence off their crops from free-range cattle. But easterners had seen Bierstadt's paintings and expected a lush garden, ready for tilling. It was a pretty tricky move.

When they arrived, though, they rose to the occasion. They irrigated the desert, diverting river streams into prairies and plains. In 1874 Joseph Glidden invented barbed wire, and most of the West was fenced off. From 1879 to 1890 the population of Idaho increased 600 percent.

While there were a lot of reasons for westward expansion (the hope of a quick fortune likely topping the list), I suspect romance played a pretty big part. The government had told a careful and lovely story. It had played to people's tendency toward big, sweeping beauty. And eventually the settlers knew what they were in for. Word of the tough land had to travel back. But people couldn't resist what they'd seen—big mountains and wild rivers and full skies. Visions like that are hard to shake.

Those months in Boston have condensed to a few mostly pleasant memories: weekend trips to Cape Cod with its grassed dunes and bleached beaches; the smells of a crowded subway train—aftershave and hairspray; cobblestone shining in a late summer rain; my first taste of matzo, paneer, lox.

In general these memories are faceless, nearly depopulated. I remember books and meals more sharply than people. But there are also fragments of conversations, always unified in a fundamental confusion. One classmate, his mother a linguistics professor at Skidmore College, said he'd love to drive to Idaho one weekend. When I told him he'd need at least three days to get there, he responded, "Bullshit. It's by Michigan, right?"

Or this: on a campus lawn after a poetry reading, I wore a cream silk dress and bare feet, my pinching high heels stuffed in my bag. I sipped white wine not because I liked it but because it was what they had. A circle of writing students said where they were from—Brookline, Manhattan, Brooklyn. I said Idaho, and a woman who was enjoying an Ivy League education, said, "Ah, a Southern belle!"

The conversations I recall most sharply are the ones that ended with me feeling countrified and like my home wasn't worth knowing. More than likely, this was insecurity talking, mistaking their forgivable geographical confusion for personal dismissal. But still, I stood there fake-sipping wine I didn't like, sweating in my dress, toeing bare feet through the grass, trying to feel comfortable and failing.

After the reading I went home and pulled a beer from the fridge and stared at that ad taped to the door, that house surrounded by land as wide open as an invitation.

It's hard to accept that the place that grew me (knowing that we are all products of place, that place and self are loyal sisters) is either skippable or shameful. Blew said, "I, who have suffered the contradictions of double vision, of belonging in place and out of place, feel a magnet's pull into that everlasting tension." It was the desire to know the world outside of Idaho that landed me in Boston, and it was the need to understand the place I'd left that drove me back.

After *Bone Deep in Landscape* I began a steady diet of western reading. In William Kittredge's *Hole in the Sky* I found another story of family, history, land. Kittredge's grandfather ran a ranch the size of Delaware in southeastern Oregon. He learned to drive a tractor and tend a harvest. He was a man, it seemed, ruddy from sun and deep-voiced from whiskey. Like Blew, Kittredge interrogated the story that drew people west, and I liked what he had to say. But more than that, his book conjured people who spurred horses and drank hard, farms that were passed down like a favorite gun or wedding ring, prairies that burned with sunsets. Those western memoirs transported me.

Worth confessing that the Kittredge quotation near the front of this book is a fiction of my own (or at least a possible misquote). At some point in college—years after I'd left Boston—I attended a writer's conference in Denver. William Kittredge led a panel about the West's mythology: people as tough as the land they tend; Edenic meadows and white-faced mountains; wild adventures and quick fortunes; outlaws and sweetheart women; spaghetti westerns; dime novels. They went on about how that story has always been a fabrication, a narrative crafted to fill a void. At the end of the panel, after everyone agreed the story of longhorns and buffalo and brave white travelers was flawed and (they hoped) dead, the panelists took questions. Hands shot up. People asked about literary influences and favorite novels. The writers all leaned to their mikes. "One more," the mediator said. I raised my hand, and when she pointed, I stood. I asked Mr. Kittredge—tired and ready to be done with us—why, precisely, the myth is so dangerous. I wanted to know what happens when we put faith in the wrong story, when we mistake fiction for fact. The room went quiet. People turned and stared. One panelist looked at her watch. Kittredge cleared his throat. I flushed at the sound of my voice; the silence suspended and throbbed until he finally said something, flatly and directly, to the effect of "If we don't evolve, we die."

In his book *Who Owns the West?* Kittredge dissected the relationship between story, evolution, and death. He explained, "We operate in systems of story and metaphor that we use to define the world (both natural and social) for ourselves, and we must always seek to remodel the mythology (model) we have inherited from society (because each synthesis always fails)." He said stories are necessary; they create meaning (à la Mary Clearman Blew), but they also ultimately give out. Here, in the myth's failing, I am most intrigued. "Stories are places to live, inside the imagination . . . and we're in trouble . . . when the one we inhabit doesn't work any more, and we stick with it anyway." Stories fail because places outgrow them. They fail, invariably, because places (and their people) change and the stories do not always change with them.

We tell ourselves stories to live. We tell ourselves stories as a way of understanding ourselves. And if we tell ourselves the same stories for too long we die. I am left to wrestle Kittredge's prohibition, to consider the dangers of this delusion, to hold the myth up to the light and trace its bifurcations and cracks. I am left to wonder where I might go from here.

The plane filled with light, and the flight attendant offered me a cup of coffee.

"No thanks," I said.

I closed my window shade and put down the Ginsberg collection and shut my eyes. I saw elk and jimson prairies and the churning eddies of the Payette River. In that moment I entered a lineage of western dreamers: my parents before me; Bierstadt before them; the Manifest Destiny men before them; Humboldt and Powell and Lewis and Clark; before them, before them, before them—another in a long line of interlopers.

Anywhere, USA

My sister Becky's house is one of those vaulted ceiling, bay window, looks-like-a-home-in-a-life-insurance-ad numbers. Doric columns and brick and river rock and a roofline that peaks at six different points. Maple trees line the driveway; a thick yard sprawls on each side, chemical green against the dusted colors of high desert—tawny cattails and pale skunk cabbage. The yard is a modern marvel: in a snap, store-bought turf rolled over saged prairie, the transformation instantaneous. When standing in her lawn, toes curled to the soil, I am struck by the coolness beneath my feet; the sharp smell of fresh paint; the blur of chandelier prisms kaleidoscoping in the front windows. It is neat and pretty as a *House Beautiful* cover.

When I'd left for Boston not even a year earlier, the yard was a horse pasture, deep with crabgrass in summer, packed with frost in winter. After thirty years of mares foaling and geldings grazing, my father dug up the field. My brother-in-law pounded nails, spread tarp, stacked beams. The rhythms of hammer on wood, lumber slapping lumber.

In the way a kid returning (or dropping out, as the case may be) from college sours when her bedroom has been changed into her mother's craft room, I was none too pleased to find the new house. This revealed a spectacular hypocrisy on my part—for my sister the new house didn't function so differently from that NYT ad taped to my fridge—but now it seemed like I had left Boston for one thing: my mare, a black quarter horse with a blaze on her nose named Misty, grazing that field, the horizon unbroken by skyscrapers or roofline. As a kid, I'd ridden Misty along the fence line, trotted her from one end to the other, led her to irrigation ditches and let her drink. At the hill's highest point, sitting loose in the saddle, I'd cup my hands to my face and holler, waiting for my voice to reflect off the foot-hills. We rustled quail and pheasant and killdeer from the brush. Once, on the bank of the ditch, I found a nest of turquoise eggs.

I looked at the horse pasture, converting so quickly to a yard, and was overrun with nostalgia. I saw only my younger self trotting my horse up that hill. But this was, admittedly, kind of bullshit. Misty's back swayed in that telltale, old horse way. She wasn't taking any-body anywhere. The young, though, can be resistant to this kind of logic. Plus, I didn't literally want my horse on that hill. I wanted to access the emotional space, the feeling. I wanted the ability to return to what I'd done in my youth. I did not want change.

The house didn't just offend my desire for a childhood preserved. Growing up, I learned that to love the West meant to hate devel-opment. But development is arguably what this region is most marked by (mining camps, frontier towns, free land, cheap land, tract houses built fast and spreading metastatically). So maybe to love a place is to own it, to insinuate ourselves into it, to change it. My family has proven this much.

In 1977 my parents bought ten acres of horse field in a farm town in the Treasure Valley, so named by the chamber of commerce for the "treasure chest of opportunities this land promised." Even the nomenclature rings with the old story: opportunity, prosperity! And this is what my parents saw.

Picture cheatgrass, a one-mile downtown with a slaughterhouse and a century-old mercantile shop selling bandanas and corn liquor, State Street lined with sugar beet fields, periodic farmhouses. Pic-ture a country and western music video.

I have imagined them as the sole newcomers in town, the young couple about to bear their first child, my father lunging a colt in the corral, my mother pouring tea on the front porch, but this is only a version of truth. In the late 1970s and early 1980s Eagle's population exploded by 400 percent, mushrooming from three hundred people to twelve hundred. My parents were nonexclusive members of a whole gang of newcomers.

The boom kept booming. In the 1990s the Treasure Valley became a mini–Silicon Valley. Tech companies cropped up, and compared to California, housing was affordable.[1] Tract houses sprouted everywhere and brought all the clichés with them: stoplights and widened highways and strip malls, the Gap and Macy's and Jamba Juice. Not surprisingly, my mother (who had come here for her horse field, her farmhouse, her farm town) spearheaded a protest against the suburban development.

After her efforts to block Walmart and Starbucks failed, she turned the fight even more locally. Her back porch bordered one hundred acres of mint owned by a millionaire named Robert Richter. The richest man in town, Richter is said to have invented wax milk cartons and TV dinner trays and the holes in Band-Aids (though this has never been confirmed). In 1990 Richter proposed a subdivision that would bury the mint farm beneath five hundred homes lined garage to garage.

Weekly, my mother camped at planning and zoning meetings till midnight. Richter represented New West development, progress, an evolution away from Eagle's rural roots toward a faceless suburbia; and my mother embodied an unwavering (and romantic) devotion to the land, to mint ripening in late summer. No one bothered to remind my mother that though her home sits on ten acres and she opposed a subdivision of fifth-acre lots, she was part of this latest development. Granted, scale and impact are issues here. One house per ten is different from fifty per ten, but on some fundamental level my mother and Robert—both

New West homesteaders of sorts—were sitting knee to knee in the same boat.

Despite her status as a relative newcomer, her protests were heard. For a long time she won.

Land battles are in this place's bones. When homesteaders fenced off the prairie—saved by barbed wire, the stuff strung as far as the eye could see and howling in the wind—open range cattlemen lost access to grass hills and mountain creeks. Their steers' ribs poked through; udders ran dry. Cattle starved. Herds dropped dead. In 1883 the Fence Cutting War broke out, and in less than a year, the cowboys vandalized over twenty million dollars worth of fence. But their fight wasn't a romantic one. My mother, refusing a development she was a part of, was spurred on by her love for the idea of the West—its snow-slumped mountains and buck-brushed plains. The cowboys' battle, like Richter's, boiled down to cash. So they harnessed their horses, cutters ready, and unclipped the West.

Becky's house took months to build. Perched in his backhoe's cage, my father levered the steely jaw into the ground—mountains of dirt displaced, cheatgrass and star thistle and wild lilac uprooted. He lay sheetrock, caulked joints. The sun dropped, the heat thinned, electrical drills squealed into the night.

As my parents dug up the far end of their pasture, development of Richter's mint field finally began. My father's backhoe churned in unison with the construction team ripping up the farm to the south. The sounds of soil turning, of earth in revolution. After two decades of fighting, Richter—worn down with age and maybe just over it—sold the farm. When a California developer bought the land, my mother, equally tired, stayed quiet, and just like that, a twenty-year battle ended with a whimper.

The mint field is now a development named Rio Bellisimo: Tuscan Living. The homes are million-dollar, mini-mansions. After hearing of my mother's antidevelopment tenacity, the developer offered to use the lot bordering her home as a park. A pond sits between my parents' faux farmhouse and the pseudo-Italian villas of Rio Bellisimo. My mother is thankful.

Like me, my sister and her husband had tried life outside of Idaho. For two years they lived in a small town in New York's Adirondack Mountains, where he taught high school math and she worked for the county, and sometimes black bears swiped berries from their yard. I don't know why she returned. Maybe she realized—pregnant with her first child—the benefits of next-door grandparents. Or maybe she was drawn by that familiar romance: a view of Shadow Butte from her kitchen window, the Boise range from her bedroom, the Owyhee Mountains from her backyard. Or maybe she had felt as out of place back east as I had.

Instead of ranching and farming, development has become Eagle's industry, and industry—as is so often the case—has become its identity. When I think of the dominant model of this place, it's the workers who come to mind—cowboys and miners and farmers. Now Idaho ranks tenth in the nation for most realtors per capita. These mini-mansions are big business, and the agents make a killing off five-thousand-square-foot palaces. Homes as massive and ornate as Becky's are the Eagle standard these days. Exempting the celebrity getaways in Sun Valley (Hemingway's last pad, Schwarzenegger's ski chalet), some of Idaho's most luxurious living is in Eagle: subdivisions flanked with angel-shaped shrubbery and fountains spurting water in little, timed pulses; houses with mini-jungle atriums.

These mega-subdivisions have become conceptual, each promising some aspect of the old story: escape, adventure, solitude. Rio Bellisimo is, arguably, the least imaginative and most misplaced. The subdivision on the other side of my parents' home postures as a Tuscan oasis: homes with marble floors and statues of armless women, cement cupids, bulbous topiaries. Homes are called "villas," and each features a seashell-colored balcony and Spanish tile roof and stucco facade. One even has an art gallery.

Like those Bierstadt paintings sent east, Rio Bellisimo promises escape. But instead of embracing the golden hills of the Treasure Valley, it asks its residents to imagine these hills are the vineyard-lined bluffs of Tuscany—an escape more distant, more exotic.

In that tired promise I see a failure to evolve.

But there is an evolution, sort of. It's no longer enough to picture Idaho itself as an escape (because we know, perhaps, that Idaho isn't some majestic Bierstadt painting made manifest). Now the escape relies on Idaho posing as Italy, and it all rings weirdly false (or not so weirdly since Eagle, after all, isn't really Tuscany—the imitation is the weird part). So Eagle's evolution should create its own story, not an Italian knockoff story. I don't want this place's narrative to become like a fake Louis Vuitton clutch sold from a car trunk.

In high school Eagle kids would drive deep into the foothills to drink beer and spin their truck wheels in the mud. Bonfires and pickup beds and dancing in the headlights. No ID checks or patrolling parents or cops tapping on car windows. Now my nights were quieter but just as restless.

At the Gap I folded jeans and gift-wrapped infant pajamas and helped women my age select dresses for job interviews or first dates. I memorized the pulsing, grating pop music that blasted through the store. When I got my first paycheck, I celebrated by taking the escalator to Dairy Queen. I sat on a bench and ate my Oreo Blizzard and wondered how many hours I had logged in the Boise Towne Square Mall. When I was five years old, my mother took me to the Claire's two doors down and had my ears pierced. Afterward, to sate my cries, she bought me a Dilly Bar from the same DQ. Now the lunch break was a long hour to fill. I dipped a fry into the shake. A pack of preteens whizzed by in a cloud of chatter and perfume, and I ached with familiarity. The ice cream slid over my tongue. My mouth burned with cold. I was, I knew, playing a long ninth inning.

After work I left the mall and bought a burger from a drive-thru and drove past strip malls and tract houses, through Eagle's downtown, past its river shore. I drove by the dirt lane that ends at my family's red barn, splitting left to my parents' home, right to my sister's. My father would still be on his backhoe, my sister and mother deep in a conversation that would turn to the new house or—worse yet—gentle proddings about what I might be thinking... *about, you know, your future?* Skip that. I drove deeper north, where the houses sit on yawning lots of land, toward that clearing in the hills where I'd burned through so many teenage-fevered nights.

When the sun sets, everything gets louder. Cicadas and bull-frogs and cows mooing. I rolled down my windows and blazed past a dairy farm, a stretch of corn. At that clearing where kids once passed out in their pickups, two stucco towers blocked the turn, an iron gate hanging between them, clenched shut like teeth. I pulled over. A plastic cubby held slick brochures: *Dynasty, Recreational Living*. This would be the nation's first "life-sport community" (a term I don't understand and which remains undefined by the Dynasty press team). Nearly six hundred acres would offer homes for people dedicated to physical fitness. Mark Spitz would open a swimming pool. Andre Agassi would run a tennis court. Glossy photos showed tanned men high-fiving on a golf course. Come to Idaho to raft rivers and hike canyons and be an outdoorsy badass, the myth has always said. But now these guys, in their pressed khakis and just-whitened teeth, are weak sauce. Swing a nine-iron, swim the butterfly, invite the neighbors for a cocktail. The old story's been repackaged, maybe even wussified. Even if the men didn't seem too refined for the story I am used to, golf and tennis and swimming aren't specific to Idaho in the way hiking Hells Canyon or kayaking the Salmon River are. Dynasty clings to the old part of this story (adventure), but it uproots that story's ties to this place. We can golf or play tennis anywhere, so the story has become totally generic.

I drove on. Thirty miles past Dynasty, beyond a pen of longhorns and a hayfield gone to seed, sage and cheatgrass blurred outside my window. Nothing but wide sky and hills the color of deer hide. Then a rare patch of chemical green: insta-grass carpeting one side of the highway. A lamppost. A sidewalk. A WELCOME TO SECRET WATERS sign. I turned.

Secret Waters is both the most traditional and most bizarre concept subdivision. It's not just a collection of similarly designed homes, nor is it a neighborhood that revolves around one theme. Secret Waters is a full-fledged community, an unofficial town. Accidentally, I had rolled into the "city limits" and found a downtown with Old West storefronts, rough lumber thrown up in flat facades. Cowboy font spelled out RIVERBED MERCANTILE and PEREGRINE DINER. I parked in front of a little red schoolhouse. A Saturday night, and everything was locked up, not a soul in sight. Even the bar was closed, but a corkboard pinned with community flyers hung by the door. I looked over my shoulder. Still no one. It was as if I'd stumbled onto a movie set and any moment someone would call "Action" and men dressed as miners would rush onto the streets and then a woman with a clipboard would ask who I was with, how I got here, who let me in, and I'd have had no good answers. I unpinned the flyer and took it back to my car. The weekly bulletin had a section titled "Farm News," which detailed the Tranquil Mind Farm Class's schedule, where residents learn how to "create an amazing productive vegetable garden." And the community is putting Idaho's fertile soil to use as a vineyard (a task Rio Bellisimo's developers are kicking themselves for not thinking of, I'm sure).

But without the community bulletin bragging about neighborhood gardens and mini-vineyards, no one would have suspected such agrarian devotions. The rest of the bulletin was mostly boring—ads for babysitters and a schedule for community hikes. Fifteen minutes later, still not another person. I drove in farther. Secret Waters is divided into a clutter of boroughs, each architecturally and aesthetically distinct. The first borough, Fresh Creek, is something out of a 1950s sitcom. Homes are painted the color of cotton candy. Maple trees shade the sidewalks. Scalloped trim lines the rooftops. All the cars must have been parked in the garages. Not a single sprinkler or kiddie pool cluttered a lawn. It felt staged and severely regulated.

Each borough is this finely planned. Paradise Bluff climbs the hills and features modern, streamlined architecture. The homes have flat roofs and glass walls and look like they belong on Malibu cliffs. Twenty minutes from Idaho's knockoff Tuscany, these houses pose in a beachless SoCal. It's remarkable how many "places" Secret Waters can be. Venture downtown, and you feel as though you're walking the planked sidewalks of a frontier town. Walk through Fresh Creek, and you're on the Cleavers' lawn. Head farther still into Paradise Bluff, and you're chilling in Southern California. And because Eagle—with all its suburban genericness—is in many ways without cultural identity (the chain grocery stores, the matching houses), it has become a real nowhere, a blank slate, and so it can be *anywhere*.

From the top of Paradise Bluff, the foothills were an ocean, Boise an island of trees and light. I pulled over and finished my burger. A lone jogger labored by, the first and only person I would see. I waved, and he nodded, but before he turned out of sight, he looked back at me, idling crudely on his route. I wondered if there are ordinances about parking cars outside of a driveway or if residents' cars have permits or badges; I wondered if he knew I was only passing through. I started the car, and the hill dipped, and the street spat me back onto the highway, returning me to the strip malls and traffic lights.

In 1987 Kittredge wrote "That old attitude from my childhood, the notion that my people live in a separate kingdom where they own it all, secure from the world, is still powerful and troublesome." The myth is dangerous because it turns westerners possessive, and on some level I see this in my parents' wanderlust, my sister's home, my *New York Times* ad. I see it in my mother's protests, my disapproval of my sister's house. And I worry about our susceptibility to that story. But that's just the first dilemma.

For Kittredge the old model perpetuates dangerous ideas about ownership and entitlement. For me that model promises (perhaps just as dangerously) individuality. When I look to my home and see a place struggling to form its identity, the story promises an easy answer. According to the old story, to be a westerner means something. It means you're tough, resilient, adventurous. Think of the explorers sending paintings east, the settlers stringing barbed wire, the ranchers tearing it down. It means you're determined. A tough son of a gun. A regular cowboy. But more fundamentally, it means you're someone with a heritage, an identity. And here I am most susceptible.

Describing Eagle, Mayor Steve Guerber coined the term *rurban*, as in, rural-slash-urban: "Eagle is a community that's maintaining its rural charm in the otherwise increasingly urban setting of Southwestern Idaho."[2] Clearly, this "rural maintenance" drives developers to repackage the old story (which in itself marks a failure to evolve), and as a result, Eagle doesn't form a new, captivatingly unique story (which is to say unique identity). At best Eagle steals other places' identities—the most obvious example being Rio Bellisimo's hulking Tuscan villas or Secret Waters's Malibu-like rancheros. Or it settles for a could-be-anywhere suburban identity—the same strip malls and box stores that line a million other streets in a million other towns all throughout America.

The problems with suburbanism are unending (developers chew up farm fields overnight, residents live far away from grocery stores or the places they work and are bound to their cars, burning fossil fuels at every turn; such sprawled living rarely supports public transportation, which creates every order of social injustice, giving the car-less few opportunities to commute to better jobs). And consider the names of Eagle's subdivisions: Secret Waters, Rio Bellisimo. Weird choices given their backdrop is droughted-out high desert. Developers conjure images that compensate for what we lack, thereby risking a whole mess of identity confusion and delusion. But perhaps what is most problematic (or at least most relevant) is that if Eagle has evolved into a suburb, then that suburb must offer its residents a new story and identity, and I'm not certain suburbia can do this. Suburbanism is all about homogenization—of place, people, culture. And if this is an evolution, then I fear it's the worst kind. People need story (as has been said) to define their world and their place in that world, which is to say to define themselves. They need story to create an identity. And if suburbanism is all about de-identification (see Idaho posing as Italy or swapping Payette rafting trips for tennis matches), then isn't this the most impotent narrative? Isn't it totally useless?

Kittredge said, "Too much order and artificiality makes us crazy." I sense that somehow he is speaking directly to Eagle. Isn't order (all those housing tracts, the matching mailboxes) and artificiality (the faux-marble statues lining Rio Bellisimo's lawns, Rio Bellisimo itself) the definition of suburbanism? And maybe it's this genericness that keeps my mother and me gripping that old story; maybe we know the reality (with its order and artificiality) fails us. Maybe an outgrown myth is better than the anonymity of suburbia.

Or maybe romance is to blame for all this unease. If it was romance that prompted me to buy a one-way ticket out of Boston, then maybe it played a part here too. Maybe if I could shrug the myth's pull, I could enjoy the shiny, convenient suburbs (the unfurling rosebushes, the suv-hoarding garages, the consumer-binging glory of Target!). Maybe my mother could've accepted Richter's Levittown a little more easily. Maybe the space between the romantics and the myth-blind suburbanites wouldn't be so wide. And maybe (in a turn severely problematic) this romance is a way of staving off evolution. Maybe it's rendered me skeptical of any transformation that would carry this story and me forward.

I think of William Hazlitt, who said of Charles Lamb, "Mr. Lamb has a distaste to new faces, to new books, to new buildings, to new customs . . . He evades the present, he mocks the future. His affections revert to, and settle on, the past." I am no better. Though I see the need for a new, true story, I'm able only to see the ways in which these new stories fail. I am like a lovesick widow, dismissing suitors over belly paunches or Celine Dion fanhood. Maybe I am only able to nitpick and refuse any and all evolution (halfhearted as it may be); maybe I foot-stamp and wait for something better, something as intoxicating as the original, or maybe just the original itself. Maybe I keep my neck craned backward, longing for (and maybe even demanding?) a story I know is better left behind me. Maybe, if I could quit this romance, mint farms and horse fields wouldn't haunt me so.

Like all industry, after a good long run, a drop-off is inevitable. Peaks and valleys, ebbs and flows. That jazz. By summer's end Eagle's development boom fizzled. Stalled by a limping economy, Dynasty didn't get off the ground. Marc Spitz and Andre Agassi never showed. The entrance to the subdivision is the largest in Idaho. Those garish towers cluster around the iron gate. Footballs and golf clubs and tennis nets etched in bas-relief into the stucco walls. Inside, ribbons of pavement slice through gone-to-seed fields. A pit for a pool remains uncemented; a tarp half-buried in the ground balloons with the breeze. Windowless homes line one side of the street. A few are half-built, their lumber bones warping in the summer sun. It's the same story all over town: cement foundations, empty cul-de-sacs, weeds pushing through pavement, ghost towns.

On the other side of my parents' fence, Rio Bellisimo's stucco mansions remain empty. The building bubble popped, and now nobody can afford these villas, with their art galleries, their cobblestoned walkways. Each night my parents weed their garden and feed their chickens, and beyond the barbed wire, Visqueen flaps against the half-finished balconies; tarps cover nude statues like togas; ceramic cherubs purse their lips, and only the dream of water flows. A fox that keeps after my father's chickens lives in an unoccupied garage. My mother hoses her strawberries and butter lettuce and pulls ripe tomatoes from their stems and remembers summer wind weighted with rich soil and just-baled alfalfa, the robust heft of fully blooming mint.

Those months in Eagle had been frustrating. How embarrassing to return home, unable to hack it in the big city, not knowing where to go or what to do next. But maybe just as problematic, they'd been lame. You'd think given all that longing in Boston, I'd have come back to Idaho in a ruffled dress and square-toed boots, humming to Patsy Cline. But I didn't. I came home and got that job at the Gap. For eight hours I winced against fluorescent lights and folded merino wool sweaters and dressed mannequins in bland business casual. I could have worked at D&B Supply, where my father bought salt licks for his livestock, or at some bacon-and-eggs diner thirty minutes away. I could have landed a job that carried the kind of rural charm I hankered for. Instead, I knotted my hair in a tight bun and wore ballet flats and tight skirts and led soccer moms to fitting rooms.

It wasn't just the job. After a shift I bought movie tickets in bulk. Plucky women bickered with disheveled men until they were in love. Vascular heroes leaped from rooftops and sprayed glass and bullets across screens. After a movie I pulled indie folk and electronica albums from record store bins. I ate curly fries in my car. I was any kid in any town.

I did not, after work, hike the Boise foothills. I did not fish the Boise River. I did not pace the irrigation ditches with my father or tend his garden or feed his chickens or toss hay to his horses. I did not walk the dogs with my mother or help her weed her flowerbeds. I drove the foothills for hours with no destination, bereft.

I came back west dreaming of that country song place, but I was a product of my home—as much a country mouse as a shopgirl. And life in the burbs, I'd learned, could be a real snooze, and I wanted something really specific and enchanting. I wanted to *be* enchanted.

Of course, that was asking a lot. I knew this farm town had transmogrified to tidy suburb. I knew the myth fails because it doesn't reflect this reality. It fails because it kept me dreaming of things I couldn't have—mint fields and horse pastures. Buffalo, mustangs, prairie, all gone the way of the tumbleweed. I knew my hometown was a ten-mile-long subdivision tract. And I knew these attachments to land—my mother's long insistence on saving the mint field, my resistance to my sister's house—were nothing new. Before farm and pasture there was prairie. All our guns were smoking.

I knew, too, that my return was a means of stunting my own progress, staving my own evolution from child to adult. How typical, that late-teen pining for her adolescence, huffing at time's natural tendency toward change. And if I'd returned hoping to understand how this place reflected me and I it, I'm not sure I got any good answers. But I was almost twenty, and the world felt crushingly small again: my parents' cramped ten acres, Eagle a matrix of tract houses and McMansions and strip malls I had memorized. I quit my job at the Gap. I researched colleges outside of Boise. I packed a duffel bag again.

By midsummer the house was finished, and when my sister asked about paint colors or patio furniture, I told her pale blue would be nice, wrought iron is classic. Maybe she, like me, felt daunted by her new phase in life—wife, mother. Maybe she just wanted the comforts of home. Or maybe we were both susceptible to old stories.

Spring had slipped into summer, and dusk dawdled till 10:00 p.m. I'd sit on the porch, watching the horses tail-swish through pasture, listening to the bullfrogs moaning from the pond. I'd think about college, wonder where I'd go, if I'd stay once I got there. I'd think about Seattle or Portland or maybe Idaho still, just farther up, in the greener, damper end of the state. I'd think about heading north up the highway, the maze of subdivisions disappearing behind me, the road long with possibility. And with all that future unrolling ahead, I'd think of Rio Bellisimo's tiled rooflines—peaked and recursive as the foothills themselves. I'd sit on the porch and look to the west, to my sister's plush lawn, her thriving geraniums, her blooming apple trees, and I'd remember how the low sun used to set the cheatgrass pink.

But sometimes there was a sweetness that wouldn't be denied. Children sticking close, fathers tossing hay, mothers rocking babies on porches, unnaturally picturesque, its glory nearly impossible, like the myth itself. My parents share the pasture, still the bulk of their property: six of the ten acres. Beyond the garden sits the chicken coop, and always there is at least one steer grazing with the horses. In the summer my niece shucks corn, my father grills T-bones, my mother plucks mint. They live off their land as much as they are able. After supper Becky and Alex walk home to the other side of the fence, their daughter cheek-down on her father's shoulder, asleep already. It is something of a dream they tell me.

How Lady Antebellum Wrecked Country Music

A (Countrified) Introduction

I order a whiskey on the rocks and press it to my neck. In this heat my hair sticks to my cheeks, my fingers swell; I am a puddle. It is August in Tucson, and the bar's patio is packed.

Despite the swelter, I wear cowboy boots. My feet pulse in them, but they are worth the discomfort. I love these boots. Love the way they point at the toe, the way they give me an extra two inches, the way they clack brightly on pavement. And when people ask where I am from, I say *Idaho*, and they say *Nice boots*, and I say *You bet*.

I think of that evening on the Boston quad, that girl barefoot and sweating from nerves as much as the heat. She is a figment.

In the desert I miss all the same things: bright frost and snowpack and summer winds smelling of cut hay and horse sweat and saddle oil. And I still worry about Eagle's proliferating suburbs, am still unsure how Idahoans are supposed to find a unique identity in a place that's becoming increasingly homogenized.

In some ways I've felt distanced from my home: I don't jibe with Idaho's conservative politics; I don't mountain bike or dirt bike or hunt elk; I haven't taken a horse into the mountains in years. But in Tucson parts of my identity feel true to the western archetype. I drive a pickup truck, wear cowboy boots, say *Idaho* with pride, and when people think my home is in the South, I understand the confusion; my clothes are more Nashville than Northwest.

My indulgence in this western clichéing is not deliberate. After I quit the Gap, I enrolled at University of Idaho in Moscow, three hundred miles north of Eagle. Surrounded by out-of-staters and Idahoans (farmers, ranchers, suburbanites, lip-pierced Boise North Enders), I settled in. I'd never been to that end of the state before, so I was away but not completely. I was home, but I wasn't. Here I could see the West in the enchanted light of an outsider. The college campus is a real stunner (oak groves and brick arches), and downtown is three blocks of coffee shops and used bookstores and one really delicious gyro joint. Northern Idaho is still mostly farmland and wilderness; wheat fields, gold before harvest, roil in the wind; beyond the farms, the hills are wooded; farther north Lake Pend Oreille is deep and clear and biting with cold. Whatever rural affection had sparked in Boston burned hot now.

In Moscow my dreamed-of West felt more intact. On the south end of town—after the clutter of campus ended but before the farm fields took over—the Plantation had cheap beer and free popcorn, and there were more locals, with their camo hats and faded jeans and polished, massive pickups, than college kids. Women wore boots and big hair, and the music was always queued to country. It was the kind of place that kept an ejected minivan seat in the corner so when folks hit their limit, they could seatbelt themselves upright. The kind of place that ran hazy with smoke. The kind of place that smelled like spilled beer and sawdust. Thursday nights were karaoke nights, and Jett, a farmer who'd lost his arm in a combine accident, had a state-of-the-art karaoke machine, and if somebody picked a Kitty Wells song, he'd two-step with you. I hardly missed a Thursday.

After two years in Moscow, I married a man with a pickup and thick beard who loves John Prine and Conway Twitty. A man who fly-fishes and backpacks and wants to, any chance he gets, isolate deep in the woods. A man who seldom misses final Jeopardy and always dishes my plate first. When we met, Ryan was earning a doctoral degree in classical guitar performance. I'd read on his couch, and he'd practice Bach lute suites, and when we got hungry, he'd cook jambalaya or grill sausages or bake salmon. It was easy to imagine a life with him.

We fell in love against Idaho's most stunning backdrops: the Sawtooth Mountains, the Bitterroot Mountains, the Payette Forest. We hiked to high lakes and swam in the clear cold. We jumped off rocks into slow rivers and broke out of the current and jumped in again. We slept in wild grass, on hot sand, in the back of his pickup parked always someplace new. Whenever we could, we left the strip malls and highways for the quiet of a mountain trail. Falling in love with Ryan was, in a way, falling into a deeper love with this place.

We got married in a mountain meadow and spent our newlywed years in that little college-farm town, eating huckleberry toast at the Breakfast Club, camping along the Clearwater River, singing songs about weeping willows at the Plantation on Thursday nights. I learned that I liked the folk music he played in his truck, the trout he fried in his skillet. That I liked the way my legs look in Old Gringos. That I liked ordering a seven and seven even more than I liked drinking it. Like the boots, the drink felt tough, unexpected from a woman maybe, and this unexpectedness—all of this—was a quick thrill.

The graduate writing program I've enrolled in is thick with easterners, people who'd gone to private colleges in New York, New Jersey, Connecticut (one poet a student I'd known at Emerson). Though I am physically still in the West, socially, this is a do-over, a chance to stay put and not scare. So I wear my boots and drive my pickup and play Loretta Lynn for anybody who'll listen.

A week into the first semester, in a fried chicken shack—the floor spotted with gum, sticky with spilled soda—I eat with a graphic memoirist from Connecticut. She points up and listens.

"Isn't this like Garth Brooks or something?"

I listen. The song is a sorrowful, smooth ballad; a man and woman do vocal gymnastics around each other. A piano plinks in the background. Though there's a mild twang in the singers' words, the song is more Celine Dion than Brooks.

I shake my head.

"But this is the kind of thing you like, right? It seems very *Idaho*."

The single is catchy, sure. A man and woman belt out the chorus, each vowel a slow, countrified drip. But the song drowns in overproduction, layers of guitar, auto-tuning. And I bristle a little at the suggestion that this is *Idaho*. In what way, I want to ask? The man whines "I need you now" one last time, and the woman whispers vocal flourishes, and the piano closes us out.

The single is called "Need You Now," and after that first encounter in the chicken shack, I hear it everywhere—in line at the bank, seeping from someone's car at a red light. And then, on a listless Saturday squandered by channel surfing, I see the group for the first time. Glowing from the television screen sits a woman with Farrah Fawcett hair and fist-sized bangle earrings. On her right a short, brunette man slouches away from the camera; on her left a long, blond man squints to the screen—a too-cool recognition of his televised audience.

The week before the Fifty-Second Grammy Awards, Chris Harrison (most widely known as the shoulder-to-cry-on host of ABC's dating show *The Bachelor*) sat down with Lady Antebellum, a country pop band based in Nashville, Tennessee. The group had released their sophomore album, received a slew of Grammy nominations, and prepared to perform at the event. A year earlier the Grammy folks knighted Lady Antebellum "Best New Country Artist/Group" for their self-titled debut album. It had been a high-earning, fame-studded year for the nascent trio.

The trio perched on barstools while a green screen of the LA valley flickered with automated lights behind them. After lauding the group's year of accomplishments, Harrison asked, "I don't mean to make you nervous, but what do you bring to that show this year? Because it's not just country. It's everybody in that room." The musicians paused. Mr. Harrison's question bordered on rude: *This isn't just the Country Music Awards. It's the Grammys. The big time. Can you hack it?* The three members of Lady Antebellum, front man Charles Kelley, backup singer Dave Haywood, and front lady Hillary Scott, each shiny with eyeliner and pomade, nodded kindly as Mr. Harrison asked if they could bring it. Then, speaking for the trio, Kelley responded, "We're just excited to . . . represent country."

Why Lady A Matters

Many things connect us to place—local dishes (oh, for Maine lobster!), literature (Faulkner and Mississippi), sports (my husband, when he is lonesome for solitude—a more metaphorical place—takes to the water, his fly rod in hand). If I used books to close the distance in Boston, then in Tucson I turn to country music. I play Garth Brooks's *Roping the Wind* and I am six years old again, my father and I singing about a man who loved a woman and a woman who just loved men. If it was a school day, he was coming from his office, and I would watch for his BMW to pull up. He ran a one-man law firm in an old farmhouse in downtown Eagle. No specialty, he worked property disputes and real estate deals and custody battles, occasionally a flashy case that nabbed headlines. He did not belong to a firm, did not work in a big-windowed high-rise in downtown Boise. He ran his own show. If he won a big case, he did not hire paralegals or run TV ads. Instead, he'd take that money and load us into a motor home so we could wander Maine and Quebec and the Redwoods for months at a time. When I told people my father was a lawyer, I wanted to explain: But not *that* kind. Not the slick, big-city kind. Not the stern, humorless kind. If you saw him out of a courthouse, you'd think he was a carpenter or dairy farmer—all dusty jeans and chapped hands.[1]

But on workdays he wore tailored suits and a fedora that reminded me of Indiana Jones. I'd climb in his car, the leather hot against my thighs, and we'd drive home singing about white knuckles and gold buckles and the roar of Sunday crowds. On weekends I would ride in his pickup truck—maybe to the foothills, maybe with the horses trailered—and I'd roll down the window and leave my feet in the wind, and he'd crank up the volume. We'd keep "Rodeo" on repeat.

If I wake particularly listless, I turn on Faith Hill's "Let Me Let Go" (or any other song, really, from the album *Faith*), and I am in junior high school, on the cusp of a driver's license, antsy for the phone to ring. How much of 1998 did I spend fidgeting my fingers through my hair, eager for something (*anything*) to happen—a friend to invite me over, a boy to kiss me? How often did I wait out all that adolescent restlessness with Faith?

If Ryan turns on George Strait's "I Just Want to Dance with You" or "Amarillo by Morning," we are no longer in our kitchen frying potatoes or sautéing mushrooms. We are not reading on our couch. The sharp heat and too-loud neighbor fade. The whir of a busy street dies down. I am transported to the shores of Warm Lake, chilled from a dunk in the deep cold. On one of our first camping trips Ryan and I drove to central Idaho and pitched our tent in a crowded campground. We woke to fathers scolding kids for messing with tackle boxes, to Lynyrd Skynyrd cranked up high, to rogue dogs pissing on our tent. No long hike, no backcountry, no solitude. It was as uncharming a scene as you could get. But in the afternoon we walked till we found a quiet sandbar. We plunged into the water and gasped when we came up. The cold hit our bones. On the beach I rung out my hair and hung my suit in a tree and pulled on dry clothes. Ryan rubbed my arms warm. We lay in the sand and watched the lake purple with twilight. On the iPod, George sang about a love he couldn't unlearn. We grew heavy with sleep.

Country music had secured a deep and overwhelmingly sentimental place in my heart. So, when Lady Antebellum came to me with the promise to "represent country," I took notice.

The Birth of a Lady

It seems a notable parallel that just as I presented myself as a prideful Idahoan, Lady Antebellum exploded on the music scene. Surrounded by Manhattanites in Italian oxfords, I found the group's drawling warmly familiar. But for all that familiarity, I remember how I recoiled when my friend said the group seemed so *Idaho*. I dislike the single (so sappy and overproduced), and I am surprised that I am not charmed by the group's overt country-ness. They are, by their own definition, country representatives. Shouldn't I find solidarity in this?

At first glance the band's formation sounds like something from a country and western biopic, like *Coal Miner's Daughter* or *Walk the Line*. A story of just-arrived dreamers banking on luck, a story of tough shakes. I imagine it this way: long, blond Chris Kelly packed a guitar and a pair of boots and lit out for Nashville. Once there, he sang on street corners and bars, his only compensation a free basket of fries at the end of the night—just another cowboy alone on the stage. His money thinning, he called his buddy Dave. The two stockpiled ballads and boot scoots and kept playing the Nashville circuit, hoping to break through, like Montgomery Gentry or Brooks and Dunn. But as is so often the case, the pair went unnoticed.

Enter Hillary Scott. A Nashville native, Scott's parents were country singers. She knew the industry inside out, and she'd been singing since she could walk. Mostly, though, she changed the chemical compounds of the group to a universally lust-inducing mixed-sex trio. With a male *and* female lead singer, listeners could hear the estranged lovers sing *to* each other (in the way of Johnny Cash and June Carter, Tammy Wynette and George Jones). Or in perkier numbers, flirtation and banter could ensue. Hillary Scott brought a complexity and sexuality that would serve the band well.

In truth what Scott brought the group, more than anything, were connections (reference her industry-mired parents), and even this isn't the whole truth. That season of Kelley and Haywood playing for spare quarters on street corners? Unlikely. Kelley came to Nashville in 2006, just three years after his older brother, Josh Kelley, rolled into town. Josh, who is a mildly famous pop singer, gained most of his celebrity for marrying the busty, doctor-playing actress Katherine Heigl. All this to say Kelley (Charles) came to town connected. Six months after arriving in Nashville (which is enough time to rent a pad and have a few meetings with your semi-successful brother's people), he'd found Scott on MySpace, talked his childhood buddy into coming down to Nash-town, and successfully put together Lady Antebellum. Within the year the group was signed to Capitol Records, joining Katy Perry, LCD Soundsystem, and, once upon a time, the Beatles.

Another Note on Band Formation

So Lady Antebellum came to Nashville connected. Big deal. Good for them. They didn't have to wait it out and suffer like so many singers. But what gives me pause is this: from the beginning Lady A seems to have been a precisely planned, carefully packaged product, something molded into a familiar, alluring object cranked out of the Industry Machine. Like the Tuscan-inspired homes behind my parents' garden, this forgoes the risk of originality and instead banks on the tried-and-true model of something that's proved wildly popular. And maybe that's fine. Certainly, it's happened before. But in country music, fans (or maybe just I?) have always expected a certain hard-knock history, a certain paying of dues. I think of Cash selling appliances by day and playing bar gigs at night and how he came to Sun Records and asked to sing gospel-inspired songs and everyone told him *Nobody'd buy that* but he kept on keeping on till somebody would. I want country artists who rose to the top by their own volition, folks who pressed on in the face of adversity, like the homesteaders or fence cutters. But maybe this is more a symptom of my own naïveté than any of Lady A's shortcomings. Perhaps I've been too romantic.

Regarding the Album *Need You Now*

After the promise of the band's first album, the sophomore record, *Need You Now*, catapulted Lady Antebellum to major mainstream success. Not everybody gets to play the Grammys, after all. The album squatted at number one on the *Billboard Hot 100*, and three of the singles nabbed the same top spot. Four weeks after the album's release, it was certified platinum, and the *LA Times* called it "impressively well considered." They continued, "Lady A delivers an emotional punch." In the world of country pop, the group was riding high.

Not everyone was impressed, though. The *Washington Post* agreed the album's title track packs some emotional sting and that Scott's vocals are pure honey but went on to say, "The sad-drunk swirl rendered so acutely [in "Need You Now"] quickly gives way to mush on the disc's ten remaining tracks, a cluster of soft-rock tunes that boast just enough steel guitar to keep Lady Antebellum CDs in the country music aisles."

The *Washington Post* touches on a fundamental dilemma of country pop music. The label seems like a misnomer, country *pop* (really, though, isn't the broader term *country and western* problematic too? With most C&W artists hailing from the southern states and with few songs mooning over western territory, the genre might better be termed just *country* or *country southern*). But each artist that has tried to straddle genre boundaries has, at some point, heard this criticism. Kenny Rogers, one of the first country pop artists, lamented, "For country music, I'm not country enough.

Everywhere else, I'm too country." So the balancing act is tricky, I'm the first to admit.

After the Harris interview, with the group cast in the unhealthy tint of a television's glow and promising Grammy success, I listen to the album online. Though I cannot palate it, the ubiquitous single does all the things successful pop music should. Heavy harmonies plague the chorus, Scott's vocals are crystal clean (if not reminiscent of Kelly Clarkson's or, at other times, Alison Krauss's), and the chemistry between her and co–lead singer Kelley pulses through at every turn. Most important, though, the number's catchy. But spare a few inordinately long vowels and the mention of a shot of whiskey, nothing about this track feels particularly country.

Generally, the rest of the album follows suit. The feel-good, up-tempo number "Perfect Day" features more country elements than the hit single but only barely. And when Lady A isn't struggling to straddle the country-pop border, it borrows from more successful pop-rock numbers. In "Love This Pain" the main melodic motive is a hardly disguised rip-off of the Rolling Stones's "Miss You." Perhaps a more troubling comparison is found in "Stars Tonight." Here the band offers a Guitar Hero version of an AC/DC song. In the background vocalists yell *Hey, hey*, and I can only imagine them to be fist pumping. The lifting continues. The ballad "If I Knew Then" opens with a pseudo-R&B drumming pattern, identical, in fact, to Harold Melvin and the Blue Notes's "If You Don't Know Me by Now." A triple meter with muffled snare beat throughout, the result is not just mushy, as the *Washington Post* suggested, but over-the-top sweet. Kelley's too-tearful singing panders desperately to the listener's emotions, and somewhere Melvin and his Blue Notes are seriously bummed out.

Toward the end of the album, though, things perk up. Right out of the gate, "Something 'bout a Woman" is startlingly country. The song begins with Dobro, then leads right into acoustic guitar, bass, and piano, and when Kelley lights in, he is drawling his heart out.

For once he sounds more like George Strait than Rob Thomas. It is, by a long ways, the album's most successful track (though interestingly never released as a single, as far as I can tell).

In the album closer the group is back to halfhearted country tunes masquerading as pop songs. In "Ready to Love Again" Scott takes over (and really, with pipes like hers, why hasn't she sung more leads?), and though the singing is pleasant enough, the song itself reminds me of something I would have loved about ten years ago, after my first breakup, which occurred in gym class while I wore too-snug mesh shorts and the whole class looked on; I spent weeks locked in my bedroom sulking in a beanbag listening to songs just like "Ready to Love Again."

My complaints with the album aren't just that it isn't country enough. Put plainly, it isn't good enough. The appeal of country pop is not lost on me. I have seen Tim McGraw in concert more than once, and each time I have flushed at his low drawl and tight jeans. Brooks, McGraw, Strait, they are all crossover stars, and I appreciate their music deeply. But they also don't blow quite as intensely as Lady Antebellum.

And here, perhaps, is why. The balancing act is difficult. As the *Washington Post* pointed out, there is only enough steel guitar on *Need You Now* to (barely) keep Lady Antebellum on country airwaves. And when Lady A isn't doing the country thing, they aren't being original (even that golden nugget, "Need You Now," is a straight rip-off of the Alan Parsons Project's "Eye in the Sky"). Maybe that's the real trouble. It's one thing to push into pop territory; it's another to rip off pop classics, only to blend them with warbled vocals and the occasional bluegrass rhythm. While borrowing from other artists is nothing new in the pop world, audiences expect that the new interpretation at least be carefully balanced and rendered.

What's more, I can't help but hope for the ideal. Oh that Lady A would define country pop as something exciting, original, free-standing. Consider how the Beatles borrowed the melodic stylings of Chuck Berry and blended them with Motown harmonies to turn rock 'n' roll on its head. Or Radiohead. The operatic vocals and sonic layers of Pink Floyd are modernized with digitally manipulated sound, and the result is pleasingly novel. Couldn't Lady A borrow only to create something fresh? Couldn't they be less derivative?

Really, though, what I'm asking for is authenticity. I want to listen to a Lady A track and sense they wrote this song *inspired*. That these aren't just old classics repackaged and that the group isn't a carefully combined product, orchestrated by a pop singer's manager. I do not want country's biggest act to be the musical analogue to Secret Waters or Rio Bellisimo, a repackaging of an old story, something posing too hard in the shadow of a thing it just isn't. And I want to know that if they'd come to Nashville unconnected and had to hawk blenders Cash-style until they got a record deal, they would have. I want to know that they combine country and pop because they believe there is some chemistry between the two or that they feel like they somehow embody both genres or that they've thought about this combination at all.

What Lady A Looks Like Live

Despite my objections to the band's latest album, when a friend offered me two tickets to their Phoenix show (she'd planned on taking her boyfriend who was visiting from New York, figuring a country band would be an appropriately Arizona-type thing to do, but he was sick, and I liked this sort of thing, right?), I took them.

Ryan is far from a fan—of Lady A or country pop in general. Classic country, outlaw country, that's his game. For the most part he indulges my Top 40 soft spot with a smile and eye roll. When we road trip, he plays Bob Dylan, Greg Brown, so much classical guitar. His tastes, I am quick to concede, are more refined. His standards higher. But when I turn on McGraw or Brooks, he turns it up and sings along. When I bring home the tickets, he jokes, "Maybe I'll buy a T-shirt." He is, per usual, a good sport.

Lady A plays a three-thousand-seat arena, and the place is packed. Packed with nineteen-year-old girls in cheek-revealing jean skirts, mall-bought straw hats, cowgirl boots, tags freshly snipped. They come in costume. Plaid dresses abound. But no one sports Wrangler's or square-toed Justins. Instead, two-hundred-dollar skinny jeans are tucked into pleather boots. This is a standard sensation at every western event. When attending a rodeo in Idaho, businessmen wear pearl snaps for the first time; soccer moms pull on pink modeling boots. So, too, at country music concerts, attendees don cowboy hats and jean jackets. Though Lady Antebellum's country styling is subdued at best, they remain country enough to prompt this kind of rural imitation.

I wear red ankle boots purchased at a boutique in New York City's SoHo district. I wear them regularly and chose them coincidentally, with zero intention of tapping into the westernness of Lady A, but perhaps this only underscores my larger devotion to western costuming. Maybe that I wear this type of getup on a daily basis makes me even more culpable; I assert my affection for country charm always, not just in the company of country pop megastars.

While the audience comes bedecked in its western finest, Lady A eschews the boot heels and belt buckles. Spotlights swirl. Strobes flash. The trio, hands clasped, waits out the crowd's roar. Kelley, a head taller than anyone else, wears boots but the Italian zip-up variety. Steven Tyler jeans and a tuxedo blazer. His hair tousled in the pseudo-reckless way of teen heartthrobs. Haywood sports skinny jeans, a sweater vest, and a fedora and likely just finished smoking cloves outside a craft beer bar. Between them, head still cast down, her leg shaking to the beat, poses Hillary Scott. Like her bandmates, she wears black pegged jeans. A tunic of blue sequins catches the strobes' light. Her hair has been blown out to Victoria's Secret model volume, and she balances, pointy toed, in a massive pair of sequined spike heels. The guitar licks through the intro to "I Run to You," a Grammy-nominated single from their debut album, and then the band breaks formation. Where Miley Cyrus would gyrate against a pole or Madonna would claw the ground, they look up. For thirty seconds the crowd has waited for a hip shimmy or leg kick, some kind of motion, and with the fanfare of a dozing cubicle worker, they lift their heads. And that is all.

I am not asking Lady A to perform as something they're not, which would be another mode of inauthenticity, but I am asking that they not be boring. To wash a stage in red pulsing lights is to infuse an audience with a certain expectation, and it's on the performers to rise to that occasion.

Kelley sings. Scott harmonizes. They turn and gaze at one another. Haywood strums his guitar, standing a little too close to the duet, the odd man out.

During fast numbers each of them moves as if they are dancing. Kelley squats a little and stamps a foot, his head tossed back to the light, the microphone tipped above him. Never once does he seem lost in the music. Never once does he seem to have forgotten that three thousand people are watching on. Scott limps across the stage, confined to short, flat-footed steps in her massive heels. She waves one arm above her head and sometimes wiggles her knees, and there her enthusiasm tops out. Haywood may dance. It is hard to tell. He is seldom in the spotlight.

Eventually, Kelley introduces the band, which is composed of an army of guitarists (mostly electric), keyboardists, bassists, and a drummer. Though he is from Georgia, there is no trace of an accent until he says, "Dave Haywood on the gee-tar." He introduces the other three guitarists and sticks with this pronunciation each time. Similarly, Scott, the Nashville native, offers no southern accent, and I wonder about those hard Rs in their songs, how *heart* becomes a two-syllable word. Whether or not Haywood has an accent remains a mystery. He never speaks.

After the introductions red lights flood the stage, and the guitar percusses through the auditorium as the "Back in Black"–esque number, "Stars Tonight," blasts. As I expected, the trio pounds fists and stomps legs and makes like rockers, sort of. But the song, again, is too refined for real hard rockery. Beneath Kelley's quavering vocals and awkward dance moves, this attempt at rock 'n' roll feels flaccid. Despite the red-washed stage and pounding guitar solo, there is no energy. The spotlight breaks on Kelley, and he twitches his hips a little and grips the mic stand and seems uncomfortable with the level of enthusiasm expected of him. He is incapable of delivering on such a charged song.

The whole show goes on this way. In fast numbers the band members twist and kick around the stage, feigning enthusiasm, feigning rock edge. During ballads Kelley and Scott embrace in the spotlight, Haywood strumming lonesomely beside them.

For most of the concert Ryan and I slouch in our stadium seats as if we are flipping through TV channels, bored but glazed.

Halfway through the set they hit their stride. The band unplugs. The pulsing lights die. All unsuccessful attempts at stage tricks vanish. The trio stands in the center, and an accordionist, upright bassist, Dobro player, and mandolin player form a horseshoe around them. We perk up in our seats. "Something 'bout a Girl," their one unabashedly country number, fires up, and the players stand on an unsmoking stage, without roaming spotlights, and they play the song. Plain as pie. Scott and Kelley stand poised, planted, singing into the audience, not at one another. Haywood plays with the other musicians. The song, unsullied with pop ambitions, is good. Kelley and Scott, freed of any obligation to entertain as a pop artist might, forget about forced dance moves and center stage poses. They move loosely, naturally, and by the end of the song, the audience is quiet for a moment, lulled, believing.

Why Lady A Doesn't Just Cut
the Pop and Go Country

That the most successful number is the band's one true country song begs the question: Why isn't Lady Antebellum a country and western band? Clearly, Lady A does not dazzle like most pop artists. Pop fans want flaming stages, smoking cages, dresses made of rib eyes. And if there is no spectacle, they want dancing. Trapeze! Cirque du Soleil acrobatics! Make it worth the fifty bucks! Lady Antebellum cannot do this. And what they lack in pop star antics, they do not make up in looks. Nobody in the group has the soap star attractiveness of most pop singers. While these demands for beauty are illogical and misplaced (pure bullshit, really), they are, regrettably, a fundamental tenet of pop success (especially these days, when a singer's mug is everywhere—Instagram, MTV, YouTube). The reality is Lady A ain't pretty enough for pop. They can't dance or entertain well enough for pop. In the world of pop, Lady A can't cut it.

But despite these shortcomings, they did what many pop acts don't: they sang and played live. While I regretted most of their stylistic decisions, they performed in tune and cleanly. And though Kelley's voice can be whiny (even for a country singer), Scott belts it with the best of them. She wails like Tammy Wynette, lulls like Patsy Cline. Yet despite her obvious vocal talents, she was rejected from *American Idol* twice, a validation of her inability to contend on a purely pop level, it seems.

More than anything, Lady Antebellum's music and performance suffer from a split identity. Recall the Chris Harrison interview when Kelley was "just proud to represent country." Yet every decision the band has made (musically, sartorially) is decidedly un-country. There is not a cowboy boot or hat onstage. The men use eyeliner, wax their eyebrows, pomade their hair. Kelley introduces Scott as the "woman with the best heels in all of country." And she flashes her sequined pumps and says, "They're Miu Miu, and I love them." Musically, the group is more influenced (*influenced* being the kindest word for Lady A's relationship with classic rock numbers) by rock acts than country artists. As they clomp around the stage and fist pump in the red light, it is clear that Lady Antebellum has tried, more than anything, to be as un-country as possible.

While it's evident that the band could not function as a mere pop act, I cannot blame them for trying to pass. Country pop sells. As a recurrent attendee of both country pop and country and western concerts, I can attest to the financial prowess of country pop. c&w's largest acts—John Prine, Lyle Lovett, Loretta Lynn, Emmylou Harris—need a stool and a stage, a fiddle and a guitar. No pulsing lights and steam machines. But comparatively, no one attends these shows. Prine plays in small theaters; I've seen Lyle Lovett four times and never once in a three-thousand-seat auditorium. The money is in the country pop world.

And whoa, is there money. Garth Brooks, High King of Country Pop, has sold 148 million domestic units. This makes him the best-selling solo act in American history. He's sold more than Elvis. More than Michael Jackson. More than Beyoncé. More than Whitney Houston and Mariah Carey combined. Internationally, his sales are second only to The Beatles. And though Brooks is definitively country pop, he's still all drawl and cowboy hats. He is a world away from Lady A's off-kilter hybrid. But despite his monstrous success, he created Chris Gaines, his pure pop alter ego—who failed . . . miserably. As Gaines, Brooks sold just two million albums. Yikes. So maybe the crossover allure pushes beyond the mighty dollar. Maybe country artists' dream of passing has to do with being cool or hip or mainstream. Maybe like shy, acned middle schoolers, country and western artists just want to sit at the cool kids' table.

The Part Where I Tell You Why This Matters

Perhaps Lady Antebellum's members are really inspired artists, and maybe country pop feels truest to them. It's significant that the genre emerged in the mid-twentieth century, just as housing tracts spread with newfound speed through the American West, as hundred-acre farms crowded with five hundred prefab homes. The country and western way of living has become endangered, and the West I know, if it were to borrow the music world's verbiage, is country pop. The majority of Idahoans live in the Treasure Valley, that land of strip malls and barn stalls; one-ton pickups parked in cul-de-sacs; cowboy hats purchased for the sole purpose of attending rodeos or concerts; horses hitched on sidewalks; cowboy-themed subdivisions. And that pop music appeals to much broader audiences (thereby generating boatloads of cash) underscores this decline. If music is a reflection of culture, then of course country pop has outmatched country and western. Pure western—musically, culturally—hardly exists in this country.

Once, Eagle looked like a town in a Faith Hill video—Orville Jackson's mercantile with its root beer floats, a single barbershop across State Street, farmers back-slapping in the greasy spoon. But the town—like every other place—has evolved, and perhaps Lady Antebellum is a picture of that evolution. The band offers an honest representation of where we are and where we're headed, as opposed to most pure country and western artists who are so often fixated with where we've come from. The group tells the story of *now*. Mercantiles flipped for strip malls; housing tracts abutting cornfields; dirt roads paved and made wider; a trio of Nashville singers making like KISS with black leather and stage makeup and seizure-inducing lights (but throwing in the occasional long-voweled drawl); a confused mishmash of rural and rock.

A (Probably Unfair) Comparison

If Lady A is an amalgamation of country and pop, antiquated and modern, then Lyle Lovett represents a less compromised facet of country music. When I think of the ways in which Lady A has failed me—how generic their music, how lackluster the group's performance, how uncommitted to both country *and* pop they seem—I recall moments when I have been satisfied with country (pop, western, whatever) music. No one does it better than Lyle Lovett. For years my father and I would flee Eagle on a bright Saturday morning and drive to the Boise Forest, where Lyle Lovett would play in a first-rate, world-class resort owned by Andre Agassi (how New West, this pimped-out lodge in the Idaho woods). The crowds were thin. Three hundred people, maybe four. Mostly middle-aged, born-and-bred Idahoans. Some cowboys. Some suburbanites.

Like Lady A, Lovett blends genres (most notably gospel, country and western, and folk). But the result is synthesized and cohesive. While his style is varied, his lyrics are unwaveringly country. He sings about corn rows and biscuits and ten-gallon hats. And while they may be common components of Lovett's world, my experience with them is limited. I have never punched cattle through a river; I have never polished a gun; I have never blown a tire just south of Reno. But each summer I pull on my boots and drive to the mountains and spread a towel on the resort's lawn and tell myself this is an authentic western experience, that it adheres to my preestablished notions of this place, to the admittedly false idea that this is a land of bulrush marshes and dust-spangled breezes, a place where every season's summer.

Not surprisingly, at the lyric level Lady Antebellum rarely seems country. Save the rare mention of white churches and barefoot women and whiskey, the group sings mostly about breaking up and moving on and growing up. Unlike Lovett's, Lady Antebellum's lyrics reflect experiences I've actually had. There is nothing idealized about them. I know Lady A's world. It is vague and therefore universal. Think of "Need You Now." Who hasn't wanted to drunk-dial an ex? Or wade in self-pity after a breakup? People get dumped. They get bummed out. They make regrettable booty calls to exes. Perhaps then, Lady A's lyrics are inherently honest and undeniably true.

A Word on Authenticity, by Way of Definition

My affection for Lyle Lovett reveals much about my insistence on authenticity. Thus far, I have charged that Lady A suffers from inauthenticity (the bad pop rip-offs suggesting uninspired music, the phony stage presence, the problematically split country-pop identity). But in many ways Lady A is nothing but authentic. The stories they tell are universal, and therefore relatable, and therefore authentic. They are literally "based in fact," they are, by definition, "not false." And it's interesting that the *Oxford English Dictionary*'s definition serves as the near exact opposite of the definition of *romance* (that belief in something that has "no foundation in fact"). So *authenticity* and *romance* are inverses, binaries.

I should clarify. Lady Antebellum fails to authentically represent my image of this place (the myth), and in this way Lyle Lovett succeeds. Lady A is not loyal to the myth in the same way Lyle Lovett is, all his six-shooters and longhorns and honey-lit plains. But if being authentic means being loyal to fact, then can one have an authentic myth? It is like asking for the true version of a lie. And so my demand for an unflagging commitment to that model, for an authentic portrayal of something that doesn't exist, is oxymoronic at best. I realize this.

Why None of This Matters

Admittedly, country and western artists sing about a culture that no longer exists (or that, perhaps, never existed). Friday nights spent boot-scootin' or fishing under the stars are idyllic, mythologized, of course. And Lady A doesn't go there. They don't offer this dishonest portrayal. They've (mostly) evolved out of that story. Maybe this deserves credit.

But I am reluctant to afford them this. That Lady A sings about experiences I've had doesn't matter because in country music, these rules don't apply. Here reality loses bearing. I come to music—to country music especially—for a story, not for the actual. I come to gain entry to an inaccessible world. I come to access something I know is bygone. When I listen to country music, I think of my home. But the experiences those songs conjure—driving from school with my father, breaking through cold lakes with my husband—they are also, perhaps more important, rooted in the past. I have said that Lady A represents where we are right now, this minute; they embody this time of transition from a distinct rural culture to the country-wide, faceless homogeneity of suburbia. And while Lady A thrives in the current moment, Lovett points to where we've come from. He's fixated with the past, and in his lonesome cowboys and tough women, I see an elegy to a world that's disappeared.

I suspect Lovett understands his job is to memorialize. I wager he knows he's offering us a dream, that he realizes there is very little "real experience" in his lyrics. For evidence see the song "In My Own Mind." The number (one of his few singles that didn't crack the charts, which I fear might have to do with its honesty) tells the story of a man who lives in a world where he plants in the spring, picks in the summer, hunts and fishes in the afternoon, and drinks coffee with his baby in dawn's warmest light. It's a land-scape doused in sunshine, where only the best harvest rains fall, a place that exists—as the chorus and title tell us—only in his mind.

Here I see not the dangers of romance (which so often keeps us roped to a dying story) but the power. In Lovett's romance he is spurred to elegize, and the very act of elegizing recognizes a thing as dead, as gone, as worthy only of memory. So I come (roman-tically, knowingly) for the dream of wild lilac and boot-grooved porches. I come to pin down the vanished. I come for the mem-ory. I come to mourn.

Try as I might, I can't make good with Lady A. So they don't offer the dishonest vision of wild rye meadows and burned-out cowboys. They've evolved out of that story. Big whoop. Their evolution, with its rock posturing and traces of old myth, is pretty shitty. They rely on the myth loosely, like the concept subdivisions that peddle the old story, just repackaged. They drawl now and again. They throw in the occasional fiddle riff. They keep that broken-down story on life support. But here's the real rub: instead of being full-on romantic about it, instead of elegizing skipped rocks and young love acted out in the confines of a cornfield, they love it halfheartedly. They rely on it in the thinnest, emptiest way (a yeehaw here, a banjo there), and they fuse it with the bland vagaries of *now*. They fail to honor an old story in the way Lovett does, but they also fail to make our current moment meaningful or memorable. Instead, they merely bemoan the trivial inconveniences of the present. After all, people sober up, they get over breakups; the drunken voicemails are deleted. The experiences and problems detailed in Lady A songs are fleeting ones, quickly forgotten, easily recovered from, unlike Lovett, who is haunted by something that won't be so easily forgotten. One must choose the romance of *then* or the immediacy (genericism?) of *now*, and Lady A fails to pick a side. Their lyrics say *now*, but their styling halfheartedly says *then*. They cannot have it both ways.

Country music is all about the vanished. I come to it not delusionally, pretending the world of a Lyle Lovett song is real, but mournfully, to access something out of reach. And maybe it isn't just that I alone come to country music to elegize but that country music doesn't want to do anything *but* elegize. After all, isn't some art about accessing the things we can't otherwise locate—like the past, like myths?

So the group's failings are reflective of this reality's failings—they are boring (see their performance) and vague (see their lyrics)—like the suburbs themselves. The problem, in fact, lies in their authenticity. They reflect the New West too well. They embody this culture's most problematic plotlines—the limping vestiges of the old model, which are tossed around brashly, and the bland monoculture of suburbanism (another carefully assembled pop group singing forgettable lyrics about forgettable experiences). They are a too-exacting copy of this dual-hearted reality.

For all my disapproval I must acknowledge that Lady A and I are not without our commonalities. I think of my friend at the chicken shack, mid-chew, freezing at the sound of the single, assuming this is something I know, something I like. *It seems very Idaho.* Or my classmate gifting me tickets—*You like this sort of thing, right?* Lady A and I are both proud, on some level, to represent (be?) country. But I'm not sure anybody really knows what that means.

I have said that the group poses too hard in the shadow of a thing it just isn't, and here I see the lamest reflections of myself. I wear cowboy boots to shopping malls and movie theaters. I drive my pickup to coffee shops. I have laid out my costume, if you will, as evidence of my earnest Idaho-ness, and while I genuinely like these things, nothing about them is authentic. I don't haul trailers or hay with my pickup; it could just as easily be a convertible. I could wear sandals or flip-flops more purposefully than my boots. I have taken the functionality of the old world and reduced it to a stylistic flourish, like a whiskey shot lyric or fiddle riff. Maybe Lady A has been just as thoughtless, yet earnest, with its flashes of country. Maybe this should elicit empathy or grace.

After eighty minutes of air guitaring around stage, Scott and Kelley retake their initial pose—legs widespread, heads cast down, hands clasped; they have come full circle. Haywood ditches the guitar and takes to the piano. For the third time I lean over and ask Ryan, "This has to be the end, right?" After the first four notes, the audience recognizes the melody to "Need You Now" and loses it. Kelley and Scott are unflappable. Heads down, they wait. The guitar cues, and seconds before her part, Scott lifts her head. With the melodrama of a Meatloaf video, she walks to the stage's end. Offering all the sexy-face she can muster—lips pursed, eyes slit—she moans the first line. At his cue Kelley wades from the shadows, his free hand rubbing his chest and stomach as though getting through this intro is both painful and a turn-on. They pose. They belt harmonies. They ogle in the way of estranged lovers. They finish. The audience goes apeshit. They scream and whoop and stomp and clap. Scott blows kisses; Kelley waves for too long; Haywood flashes his palm once and is offstage. They disappear. The lights die.

The audience pounds, yells, begs for more.

I close my eyes. Warm Lake laps against a hot shore. Ryan lies faceup to the sun. I turn up the iPod, and George Strait sings a simple song—a guitar, a violin, maybe some harmonies. We curl against each other, Ryan's cheek in my hair. How quickly we find sleep. I see my mother's gingham blanket. On it my father and I eat crackers and cheese and share one overpriced Coors. Lyle sits on his stool, and the gospel singers line behind him. Between songs he sips water and twists his tuning pegs, and there is only the sounds of people on a lawn—a beer can crunching, a woman's high laugh, my father tapping the rhythm, gone now, on his leg. Gnats cloud in the spotlight. I lie on the blanket and watch the sun drop and feel slack and full.

All that seems far-off now.

The lights blast on again. Lady A retakes the stage, and I have seen all I can take. Three more minutes of Kelley and Scott singing rock rip-offs as though the microphone is a hairbrush and they are pantslessly wailing in front of a bedroom mirror is more than I can bear. I pick up my purse. Ryan collects our empty beer cups. As Scott and Kelley belly up to the mic, we shuffle our way down the aisle, past the wailing fans in glitter-rimmed cowgirl hats and unscuffed boots, and are turned out into the night.[2]

The Slaughterhouse

Springtime in the desert is a nuanced shifting. The locals call it blooming season, and if your eye is unaccustomed, the flecks of owl clover or Russian thistle are easy to miss—drops of pink in a wash of red and brown. By the time the school year ends, most days see the high side of one hundred. I pack a duffel bag, and Ryan drives me to the airport. He will stay here, teaching classical guitar to children in the wealthy pockets of north Tucson, and when I ask if he's sure he can't come, if he's sure he wants to wait out these blistering months alone, he is all pragmatics. *Rent's gotta get paid. No sense in both of us suffering.*

He is the only hard part of leaving. There is no pang of repetition here. I do not think of that Boston flight, the abandoned apartment still full of clothes and books, the anxiety over what my parents will say. Because I am not returning, only visiting, and I take a peculiar pride in this. I am learning a new corner of the world, picking up new words: *paloverde, Chiricahua, cholla.* I am staying put.

But by May I am antsy for the frost-glittered mornings of a high desert spring.

In northern Idaho I had leaned into my semi-rural roots. I wore plaid shirts and karaoke'ed at the Plant and ignored the fact that my childhood was just as marked by mall sprees as it was by rodeos, that my father was a New York transplant who rode horses and kept steer for pleasure only. In Tucson I am the girl to whom people unload country concert tickets, the girl who sings Old West elegies with my truck windows rolled down. I had been told to evolve or die, and I'd dug in my heels.

When I arrive in Eagle on a Saturday morning, downtown is hopping. The retail-hungry come for Thai brunch or sales at fashion boutiques, where Italian denim and handbags are priced like used cars. They come to picnic in the gazebo. They come to set fidgety kids loose in water fountained jungle gyms. They come to pinch tomatoes at the farmer's market, where produce was trucked in from Fruitland or Kuna or some other town forty minutes away, where people still farm.

The Eagle Shopping Center is a pastel strip mall with that cupcakery and a florist shop that sits on the Boise River. My sister and niece pick me up from the airport, and we stop for a treat. I order a hot latte. We find a bench by the river's shore. My sister walks her daughter to the water, and they toss rocks and point at dragonflies. I hold the coffee close. After a year in the desert, the forty-degree temp is unreal. I zip up my jacket and feel like a wimp.

The river rolls behind the cottonwoods, and the sunlight is fickle and bright on the water. It feels good to sit in the sun, to hear a river roil.

Back in the day, the river meant farmers could irrigate their hayfields and cattle ranchers could drive their herds to drink. Even into the 1980s, when I was a kid riding my bike downtown, buying bubble gum and jerky sticks, Eagle was little more than foothills and ranches and a river shore. Downtown was tiny. A barbershop shared a space with the local library. I learned to sound out *cat* and *bug* to a chorus of clippers buzzing on the other side of the door. There was Orville Jackson's Mercantile and my father's three-room law office and, on the riverbank, the biggest building in town, the Boise Valley Packing Plant. Penned by the shore, slump-backed horses muzzled dust and waited their turn. Stencils of horned Herefords faded on the cinderblock storefront. Trapped in an idling school bus, I'd watch the old mares with their hindquarters to the wind, their necks bowed.

My brother and I rode the bus with the Vogel kids. They lived down the lane and said they had, though I never counted, eighty-seven cats. The Vogel's cats were everywhere—napping in the driveway, curled on car hoods, cleaning themselves in the kitchen sink. Once, in an attempt at population control, Russ ran the cats into a pit and shot them with his BB gun. He offered the gun to my brother, who declined. Russ shrugged, aimed, and I looked away.

When the bus stopped beside the slaughterhouse, Russ would pop over the seat and say, *The meat packer's son hanged himself there, swingin' between slabs of beef.* I'd stare wide-eyed at the slaughter-house door. I'd listen for gunshots.

Like my latte, there are good things that have come from Eagle's transformation. It's a transformation that is typical of certain western towns, those close to thriving urban centers, those with beautiful snow-capped mountains in the backyard, those with major universities nearby. Granted, for every Eagle there are countless towns too far removed from a major city to experience this kind of revitalization. Push out of the valley into the high desert and find the boarded-up gas stations and single dive bars but not much else. Find the towns with the welcome signs posted on the main drag, the population number newly printed and smaller than before. Find the places growing into ghost towns.

For all of Eagle's revitalizations, I miss the slaughterhouse. The packing plant made my hometown seem like something from a movie. Think of *Cattle Drive, Red River, The Far Country, Open Range, The Overlanders, Lonesome Dove, City Slickers.* Each tells the drama of shuttling thousands of steers thousands of miles, the inevitable stop (off-screen but implied) a slaughterhouse. They tell the story of the strong, usually handsome cowboy riding months in the saddle, braving hundred-degree temps, blizzards, waterless creek beds, snake-bites, and frostbite just to move his herd to fresh meadows.

The cowboy's appeal can't be overstated. He is equal parts working hero and soap opera heartthrob. He mirrors who we want to be (gritty people who muscle through) and who we want to have (that tough-palmed, low-spoken man who softens in the night). My earliest crushes were all versions of the cowboy: Paul Newman's Butch Cassidy, Luke Perry in *8 Seconds*. The first boy to ask me to dance was a junior bull rider, and the boyfriend I missed in Boston was the son of a farmer who kept a bull in the pen, a clutter of steer in the field. We'd drive to his house and park by the corral and eat fries in the truck bed, the night loud with cattle roving, the sound of labored breathing. My husband in so many ways satisfies this model. I have never seen him on a horse, but when I met Ryan, I was struck by his slowness to speak, by his quiet voice, by his ability to wander miles deep into the wilderness with little more than a rucksack and canteen. A shy, muscle-roped man asleep by a campfire, a vision I'd harbored since I began harboring visions of men.

So I looked at the slaughterhouse and saw a western hero. Or maybe I saw an American hero. The cowboy enchants universally. After all, Americans everywhere are susceptible to Dodge Ram commercials, with their sun-leathered men hauling trailers of longhorns. And those cattle drive flicks played in theaters nationwide. Toby Keith, famed crooner of "Should've Been a Cowboy," fills stadiums all over the country. The cowboy and his calf woo all of America, so maybe their disappearance, and this enchantment with them, transcends me, Eagle, the West.

Admittedly, Eagle's history is dwarfed by those movies and my harbored fantasies. The Boise Valley plant wrapped meat brought in by small-timers, farmers or businessmen moonlighting as ranchers. Or after decades of faithful trail service, foundered horses were dropped off by bleary-eyed cowboys. Business had gone like this since 1913.

In 1996, after eighty-three years of operation, the slaughterhouse closed, and in its place a Montessori preschool and the gourmet cupcake shop and a Thai buffet sprouted up along the river shore.

In the early 1860s miners crowded Idaho, and Texas boomed as the ranch capital of America. Books like *The Beef Bonanza: How to Get Rich on the Plains* promised easterners that cattle meant cash, and for a long time the promise held. Where Texas had supply, Idaho, jammed with hungry miners, had demand. The fifteen hundred miles between the Lone Star State and Idaho lapsed into a doglegged cattle trail. And when the river pans came up empty, irrigation transformed prairies into farm ground (thus towns like Eagle, rich soiled on the river's shore, were born). And so a mining town turned to farming and ranching, just like that.

Three days after I land in Idaho, my father asks if I want to go to a cattle auction in Caldwell. He says he'll buy me a burger. I follow him to his pickup. It smells—as it always has—of dust and coffee and horsehair. The sun beats through the window, and I press my hand to the pane, thankful for the warmth.

Like so many places, Eagle has switched out dirt lanes for highways, farm fields for subdivisions, slaughterhouses for cupcakeries. No news here. I don't want to belabor this evolution or wallow in its arguable sadness. What I want to suggest is that this cattle fixation (didn't the words *cattle auction* get me off the couch?) is at best anachronistic, at worst delusional.

Outside of Eagle the subdivisions thin, and grain elevators shine on the horizon, and the next twenty miles will be farm fields— onion and alfalfa and malodorous sugar beets. Just inside Caldwell, boot shops and farm supply stores line the main drag. Longhorns and river canyons are painted on billboards. Plastic horses—shiny buckskins and buffed roans—stand hitched in the Ranch Supplies' parking lot. Tin cowboys lean against shop windows. It feels like a Disneyland frontier town.

The Treasure Valley Live Auction is a low, long, paint-peeled building that looks like a bingo hall or run-down office complex. The parking lot is full of pickups and semis and horse trailers, naturally. Just beyond the auction building, cattle and sheep rustle in stock chutes. A sign on the door reads, with little explanation, "We no longer accept boar pigs." My father parks his Ford one-ton by the main entrance. It's a workday, and so he is in his lawyer getup: black slacks, a wool sweater, still that felt fedora. His truck is without the dirt clods or kicked-in tailgate that are typical. He pulls a Carhartt over his cashmere and ditches his hat. I wear skinny jeans and a peacoat and a slouched knit beret. It is something of a graduate student uniform, and I wonder at my compulsion to dress against type. In Tucson I dress like someone driving to a cattle auction; here I look like I work in a coffee shop in Brooklyn. The cattle low as we pass.

Inside, the auction grounds are divided into three rooms. The Cattlemen's Café offers beefy tomato mac and cheese soup on special (though I find it hard to imagine eating beef in such proximity to all those big-eyed cows). At 10:00 a.m. on a Friday two men drink coffee and butter toast. They sit at the diner bar in near silence, and a woman in short jean shorts and a long ponytail stands behind the counter, rubbing spoons with a dish towel. The men eye her as she bends for fresh rags, and she pretends not to notice.

"You bidding?" she asks me, eyebrow lifted.

"I'm with my dad," I say. "He's in the corral."

She tells me she grew up in Caldwell, the daughter of a cattleman, knows the industry inside out, but now she works here, and she likes it all right because business is slow and sometimes in the afternoons, between lunch and dinner, she can sit in a booth and read *Glamour* because nobody's here and nobody minds.

I find my father in the bidding room. The corral is where the real action is. A half-moon of bleachers, five rows high, the room smells, not surprisingly, like cow shit—which is to say it smells like the hot summer wind of my childhood. I sit next to the only other woman in the crowd. She wears pink boots and a tight T-shirt. Rhinestones bedazzled across her chest read, "I suffer from PMS: Putting Up with Men's Shit."

In the corral one feeder stands alone. Coat clumped, it is downright mangy. Two men with shovels prod the animal as the man in the little box mumbles, "Sixty, I got sixty-five, six and a half, seventy, I see eighty, eighty, eighty, sold." The cow sells for eighty cents a pound. A door flies open. The outside light shocks the dim corral, and the steer flies down the chute, out of sight.

Outside, ranch hands move the cattle from one pen to another. The air is sweet and rank with cud and manure. It is Friday: feeder day. The herds of newly weaned cows are fidgety. A teenaged kid in coveralls with a blond mustache taps a pole along their rumps. The chute is clogged, not nearly wide enough for all the cattle, but they barrel through. A black steer, little rebel, kicks and leaps. It spins and runs upstream, not knowing where it is heading but wisely suspecting the corral will be even worse than the chute. The young cowhand racks its legs with the pole. The cow tries to leap through a closed gate, and its head lodges between slats. "Not real smart critters!" the boy yells. The cow twists and kicks, its neck bending at impossible angles (it is gruesome to watch), until finally it breaks free and enters the stream, heading toward the bidding floor.

Maybe five years ago, a decade even, I imagine the cowhand went to auction with his father, borrowed three hundred dollars, and chose a calf with warm breath and Bambi eyes and a muzzle soft as buffalo grass. By summer's end, the calf plumped, he returned to auction and doubled his money.

Once the Vogel kids raised a dairy cow for 4-H, but they went too long without milking it, and when it got mastitis, their father got the gun. Russ led us to the field and showed us the stained dirt where the animal fell, the air still metallic with the stench of blood. After that, I never considered raising a calf of my own.

But when I was five, my father brought home a Jersey I mistook as a pet. At dinner my brother leaned over and—mouth rolling mid-chew—said, "You know you're eating Little Dot, right?" Cue tears. But the real farm kids in Idaho learn this lesson young, and they respect the system and take pride in being a part of it. When most beef comes from factory farms and low-grade, grain-fed burger is served with bone chips in the patty, a kid grass-feeding an Angus and taking it to market is a rare moment of western idealism: aspiring cowboys, healthy cattle, small-town slaughterhouses, the myth turned reality, the myth at its best, but this is tangential.

More to the point: if a twenty-first-century cowboy exists, it is here, at the Treasure Valley Live Auction. And this is what I've come for. I have not outgrown, it seems, my affection for the quiet, solitary man who is prone only to the right woman's touch. And excepting my father in his black cashmere, these are the modern cowboys, the TVLA their cattle drive. Men gather, buy a herd, load them in a trailer, and drive back to a pasture of bluestem and salt grass. No thousand-head roundup or open range ride but a collecting nonetheless.

A collecting in the spirit of those epic roundups, sure, but to what end? As the Cattlemen's waitress so wisely observed, things are quiet around here. A few sales on a Friday morning, feeders going for cheap, taken back to a small plot, taken out of state for slaughter, and maybe, by the end, the rancher makes a little money—but only maybe.

Next week my father, motivated by the bottom line, will find a man on the internet. We will pick up a Hereford named Meg, and she will follow my father like a well-trained dog, nuzzle his arm as soon as he's near. She will graze his pasture for the next year, and then there will be a barbecue.

Despite the scant crowds at the auction, cattling remains a big slice of the Idaho Ag pie. So big, in fact, that Eagle is home to the world's largest Rocky Mountain Oyster Feed, an eight-dollar, all-you-can-eat ball buffet in the corner of a weeded, vacant lot. (Pro tip: the testicles-turned-appetizers are also known as *swinging beef*, *prairie oysters*, *dusted nuts*, *tendergroins*, *bull's eggs*, *calf fries*, and *bull fries*, should one want to search them out.) The feed is rooted in the tradition of frying bull testicles after ranchers performed their yearly castrations—though inquisitive patrons learn that the "cowboy caviar" is usually purchased frozen these days, as the only true way to get them fresh is "straight off the range," and by *range* I assume the nut purveyors mean from the holding pens of someone who still ranches . . . somewhere. But that's not to say the industry hasn't changed. For much of the early twentieth century, sheep ranches were the real moneymakers. In fact, sheep husbandry was much more influential in Idaho's economy than cattle ranching, but I seldom remember this. How can the shepherd and his flock, so mired in biblical imagery, contend with the tough—and usually sexy—cowboy? But all this industry talk only reveals a greater transformation.

When Boise boomed as a tech town, the whole state's industry changed. Now science and technology comprise 25 percent of Idaho's economy, and Idaho (known—if known at all—for its potatoes and pickup trucks and cowboys) ranks number eleven nationwide for technological job creation. Agriculture, providing so much of Idaho's identity, accounts for just 6 percent of the state's workforce. If cattling accounts for a third of that 6 percent, then overall we're talking a miniscule 2 percent of Idaho's industry.

The week after our trip to the auction, I find another iteration of the modern cowboy. The ad for the Idaho Cutting Horse Association Aged Event and Weekend Show is a ten-page insert in the *Idaho Statesman,* showing bareback riders dressed in buckskin and war paint. Fine boots, custom tack, plush saddles, will all be for sale. Oil paintings of wild horses, muscled and stampeding against a neon sky are framed in buck antlers. A bluegrass band and then a bazaar and a fair. The place will be hopping, a real cowboy get-down. I've never seen a cutting competition, but I imagine it will be something like a rodeo: elephant ears and cotton candy and flying sod and loud buzzers and up-on-their-feet fans. My father lets me borrow the truck.

In Nampa, Caldwell's twin city, cowboys and cowgirls saddle up their ponies. The cutting show is held indoors in the Idaho Horse Park, a building that more closely resembles an airplane hangar than a barn or corral. A few booths are set up in the corner: boxes of cowboy boots clutter one; neon canvases of bucking Appaloosas line another. Most of the kiosks are empty. There are no buyers, no crowds. It is a party of no-shows. It is quiet and sad.

Instead of bleachers, about twenty fans (or participants? supporters? one cannot be sure of the appropriate verbiage) sit at round tables, where they enjoy the lattes and scones from the park's Java Hut. Women with severe perms and glossy acrylic nails share muffins. They look like Julia Roberts and Dolly Parton in *Steel Magnolias*: hair-teased and giddy with gossip. Men, as flannelled-out as the ranchers at the TVLA, dab cappuccino froth from their mustaches. Industrial fans whirl overhead, killing the must of horse sweat and manure. Inside the corral a woman pulls herself into the saddle and rides toward a waiting herd. With no signal—no waving flag or cracking pistol—the clock ticks.

In the days of the open range, herds mingled. In the spring ranchers had to isolate their cows from the tangle, so they needed low-to-the-ground horses that could move more lithely than a steer.

This competition is the most overt remnant of the great spring roundups.

The woman moves her horse slowly—really slowly. It's like she's just killing time, riding in haphazard circles. Finally, she squares off with one steer. The cow bolts to the left, to the right; the gelding charges each time. Its chest brushing the sod, the horse is as low to the ground as the young steer. The match beats on: the cattle darts, the horse lunges, a stalemate. The cow can't get back to the herd, but as the final seconds drop, the steer bolts backward. The horse can't cut off its path quickly enough, and the cow escapes to the far end of the pen. If this were open prairie, the cow would be running free. The cowgirl would be screwed. On a neon sign, 40 flashes, a low score.

The sport is painfully slow: two-minute rounds with long breaks between each. The crowd chats or texts on their cell phones. One man, riding straight-backed in the saddle, scruffy jawed and hand-some as a Marlboro Man, pulls off a glove with his teeth. From his hip pocket emerges an iPhone, its lights flickering in his palm. Finally, another round begins, and almost nothing happens in the first ninety seconds, which isn't to say it isn't exciting when the horse thrashes and the cattle leaps, when the sod goes flying. Watching the animals stomp and charge is a rush for sure, but this only lasts twenty seconds—a jolt of adrenaline in a long lull of horse circling herd.

The economic necessities of a century ago have dwindled to hobby. The National Cutting Horse Association website tells me 16,442 people are members nationwide, and last year's national champ pulled down eight thousand dollars. The website boasts these figures as if they reflect a booming trend, as if everybody's doing it.

Of course, hardly anybody's doing it. As Idaho industry indicates, the cattle world is in full decline. It's the mint field razed for Tuscan villas all over again. A million places, all the same. Flux, evolution, reinvention. But accepting that Idaho's economy (identity?) rests on microchips is asking a ton of its residents. Idahoans, like most westerners, take pride in their ruggedness. See the TVLA parking lot as proof: cowboy boots stenciled on rusted-out fenders; eagle and elk and trout decals fixed to rear windows; NRA stickers everywhere.

In the cowboy we see a reflection of our imagined selves. And here, I suspect, is why Idahoans fight to keep the dream of the cattle culture alive. Our toughness has waned. We've evolved from gritty cow rustlers to soft-palmed office workers. We've traded cattle trails for fluorescent-lit, temperature-controlled cubicles. We have taken the cowboy and jacked his chaps and spurs and decked him out in Dockers and tasseled loafers.

There's no tragedy in this. But what's significant is that this world of sedans and corporate headquarters—compared to cowboys sweating horseback and open ranges—so clearly lacks the sex and desire and toughness of the old one. The cowboy romance (in both its nostalgic and harlequin sense) collides with this tame, boring lifestyle, and the reality, of course, pales to the dream.

These romantics—the cutting competitors, keeping an old tradition alive; me, the nostalgic spectator; even my father, buying a cow for fun or pride or principle but not necessity—cling to the cowboy ethos because in the Valley the memory of tawny longhorns and hard-riding men weighs so heavy there's no escaping it. Or there's no desire to escape it. Idahoans love the myth enough to perpetuate it but not enough to protect it. We allow the culture to die but then refuse the necessary evolution that takes us from the tired story of downtown slaughterhouses to the reality of Saturdays spent lounging on the river's shore, cupcake in hand, the sugar gritted on our lips.

I am the chief offender. Hadn't I waxed nostalgic over a bulldozed kill site while enjoying the very strip mall that supplanted it? I picked at my niece's abandoned cupcake and sipped my latte—in the burbs and loving it.

At the cutting competition, the failures of both the myth and romanticism become evident. The small group of Idahoans who cut herds in a cement corral is trying to access something long gone. Like me swaying at a Lyle Lovett concert, they are searching for a memory stored in a collective conscience. But they are doing it without realizing, it seems, that the industry is pretty much dried-up. In the ranchers (who are fighting their fight, trying for a living) and the cutters, there is no open acknowledgment that this world has nearly disappeared, so there is no elegy. And if the romance isn't spurring us to elegize the past, then we can only hope it is prodding us toward preservation.

This is not to suggest that we should preserve the myth as though it's a reality but that we should preserve it in the way we maintain historic buildings or artifacts, something we maintain *because* it's outdated, anachronistic. Maybe the myth could be a relic we polish and keep glass cased on the highest shelf.

But that won't work because romance doesn't preserve. Nobody showed up to watch those cowboys sort herds; the Cattlemen's is quiet and those feeders sold for cheap. So, if the romantics aren't elegizing or preserving, then what are we doing?

After enough time has passed, some argue, technology will be a cornerstone of this place's story. Try to imagine it: at Halloween no cowboy costumes; instead, kids lugging keyboards and mouse pads, explaining to friends *I'm a computer engineer, obviously.* The Old West can be mythologized, some say, because it's so removed. And don't we always prefer the past to the present? Doesn't the distance of time too often make the past intoxicating, if not infallible? But before most whites had even seen the West, it was mythologized. Think of Bierstadt sending those first landscapes back east. In 1860, before railroad connected East and West, the first western dime novel was published. In 1893, just three years after Idaho joined the Union, Buffalo Bill formed his first Wild West Show.

That story was written immediately. Mythology, then, is independent of distance and time. Somewhere between Caldwell's cattle
auction and Eagle's shopping sprees lies a new story, dormant and
waiting to be plumbed.

If we look to the cowboy for evidence of our toughness, then maybe
industry isn't as relevant to identity as I thought. After all, the cowboys are pretty much gone, and Idaho's few remaining ranchers
generally hang onto their operations by a thread (woven usually
from federal subsidies—the government actually pays to keep this
old story up and running). But we deny those lackluster techies
and swoon for our vanished hero, telling ourselves we are one and
the same. Industry, then, doesn't reflect identity. Or it should, but
we don't let it. When we find industry less than charming, we run
back to the romance of story.

   If all that talk about industry and identity is bunk, maybe that
the slaughterhouse closed doesn't matter. Maybe the thing can die
but our enchantment can persist. Like a kept-away fossil, the shell
of something gone but loved anyway. Maybe our affection for the
old story doesn't occlude the creation of a new one. Maybe we can
love the past and still move forward. Or maybe Kittredge would
tsk at all this half-assing. Maybe he'd tell us to let the old story rest.
Maybe we should look for new things to love.

After the round is over, the contenders stay mounted and watch
the next match from horseback. The neon lights in the horse corral have triggered a migraine, and my temples are bolts of pain.
The smell of horseshit is stomach flipping. Any delusions about
personal toughness have waned. I order a coffee, swallow two
pills, and close my eyes. I hear the quarter horse snorting and
sniffing its way around the herd. The cattle maw and shuffle into
each other. It is late in the day, and on the other end of the valley,
downtown Eagle is slowing. The boutiques are closing, and shop-

girls refold sweaters and steam trousers. The park is emptying. A boy at the cupcake shop flips the sign from OPEN to CLOSED and takes the garbage out back and watches minnows flit through the river shallows. He breathes deep the smell of river water, moss, skunk cabbage, daffodils, the garbage in his hand; it is sweet with stale cake and buttercream. The river teals in the late light, and all is quiet, save the sound of water coursing over rocks, a fountain gurgling behind the park bench. Dragonflies flit from the river to the fountain and back again.

I open my eyes. The cowboy cuts the herd, this time more successfully than the last contender. My coffee half-gone, I gather my things. On my way out, I look once more to the cowboy, and I don't think of the slaughterhouse or handsome cow rustlers. I return to lattes warming me in the sun, to the dream of a cashmere sweater picked from a boutique window and worn right out of the store. The cowboy looks small, his horse tired. The crowd of twenty has thinned to ten. He cuts the herd, this time more successfully than the last contender. He breaks the pack earlier, a minute in, and one steer stands alone. The cow bolts, but the horse is faster, anticipating his next move. He keeps the animal stationary, never allowing it to look back to the far end of the pen. The seconds drop. The steer is stuck. The judge yells 70, a high enough score, and in this cowboy's mind he and this steer are alone in the Owyhee plains. The sun beats hot on his neck; he smells sweat and sage and saddle oil. The only sounds to be heard the animals' heavy breathing and low snorts, the murmuring Snake River tripping beyond an unseen butte, the groan of a leather stirrup swinging, that hot wind humming through dry brush, and he leads the cow away.

Anything Will Be Easy after This

Preparation

Summers in Idaho are rodeo season. Beyond the Treasure Valley, in the hills, on the plains, in Blackfoot or Riggins or Burns, pick-ups line ditches. Women wear jean skirts and pink boots; men don hats and gloves. Slouched in the stands, they nurse Buds and share nachos. The weak-stomached grow woozy from the deep pungencies of hops and reheated hotdogs, boot polish and Old Spice. In the corral toddlers cling to bolting sheep. Cowboys ride broncs bareback. Pretty women with sashes pinned to their chests circulate among the crowd. A crown shines from their hat brims. The White Bird Rodeo Queen. The Gold Dust Rodeo Queen. The Whoopee Days Queen. In this circle the queen reigns supreme.

Rodeo queens are the princesses of Idahoan childhoods. Parents load up their kids and take them to the Caldwell Night Rodeo, the Jordan Valley Rodeo, the Snake River Stampede, and young girls come expecting more from the queens than anyone else in the show, and the queens deliver. They pose for pictures and perch on chute gates and cheer when a rider lasts eight seconds. Young girls stare on, entranced by those piled coiffures, by those blouses that shimmer in the sun.

Then, flying from the chute, a queen on horseback. Her hair waving behind her, she sprints around the ring, a strange concoction of powdered femininity and deep-muscled strength.

1. These and the other stipulations noted here have been pulled from the Miss Rodeo Idaho 2011 Contest Rules handbook, naturally.

2. Informally, boyfriends (lived with or otherwise) are frowned upon. Few queens offer a concrete explanation for this guideline. They just shrug and say, "Everyone knows to introduce him as your cousin." All the queens have cousins.

3. *Ideal*, a word worth consideration. Certainly, MRI's notions of "ideal" are very specific, though the word here remains undefined. Common definitions locate the term as something "existing as an archetypal idea" (as in, *ideals* = morals or beliefs). Or *ideal* = something "existing as a mental image or in fancy or imagination only; lacking practicality." Like a fantasy, like a myth.

   Perhaps, then, here is why I have elbowed my way into observing the rodeo queen pageant. A first-generation Idahoan, I have situated myself somewhere between the rodeo queens of rural Idaho and the California transplants of Eagle. The competition is itself a sort of anthropological experiment; they are here to locate (and thereby define?) what it means to be a certain (ideal!) type of western woman. What it means to be western and a woman is at the heart of this competition, the heart of my infatuation with Idaho, and maybe even, the heart of these pages.

Each summer the queens take to the ring. Girls truck in from every corner of the state, spurs polished, hair bleached. They compete for the state's most coveted title, Miss Rodeo Idaho, and this year the competition falls in the middle of my visit; the timing is serendipitous. I contact the MRI Pageant coordinator and explain that I am a writer exploring my Idaho roots and, consequently, rodeo queens. Summers spent in sun-hot bleachers with the staticky calls of fast-talking announcers and bull riders spinning to the sod have left me enchanted with this leather-fringed microcosm. The coordinator, in a familiar gesture of Idaho congeniality, indulges me. After a week of emails, I receive a press pass to all events, access to the girls round the clock, and the MRI 2011 Contest Rules handbook. On the book's cover is a picture of the current Miss Rodeo Idaho, Amber Jackson. Queen Amber stands next to a pine tree. She wears a crown fixed to a black cowboy hat and a rhinestone-studded leather vest. Thick makeup and red lips and teased hair add two decades to the nineteen-year-old, but she smiles on sweetly.

Criteria[1]

Must be born a female, no younger than eighteen and no older than twenty-five. Must be single. Must never have been married. Must never have been pregnant. Must not live with someone of the opposite gender who is not a relative.[2] Must hold a high school diploma (or an equivalent degree). Must not commit or have committed crimes of moral turpitude. Must not harm Miss Rodeo Idaho's reputation. Miss Rodeo Idaho is, the rulebook stipulates, "the ideal Western American young woman."[3]

The entrance fee is $450, nonrefundable. Historically, the contestants must hold a rodeo title. The process is sort of like being crowned Miss Boise and then competing for Miss Idaho. But the queens hate beauty pageant comparisons (even though MRI refers to itself as a pageant, it is not a *beauty* pageant). They are quick to

4 In truth no one is certain of the numbers. The MRI institution, run by volunteers, does not keep close records, and when pressed to discuss the obvious curtailment of competition, nobody talks. What's certain, though, is that in the rodeos of my childhood the ring was lined with MRI hopefuls. And this is the first year the MRI institution has accepted non-title-holding competitors. Clearly, things don't look so hot for the MRI circuit.

5 Regarding gangs, kind of. Some stop signs are spray-painted. As for the bad smell, this claim is less arguable.

6 The family stipulation makes sense. Like beauty pageant contestants (apologies for the comparison, queens), rodeo queens' mothers can be overbearing. Most girls began queening before they learned to read, and their mothers have been instrumental in teasing their hair, painting their nails, and quizzing them on horsemanship trivia. MRI makes a point to exclude this kind of influence.

point out that nothing they do requires a bathing suit. The queens consider themselves more analogous to cheerleaders. They promote rodeos much in the way a cheerleader promotes a football team. And both require major doses of athleticism. They do not, however, "prance around in skimpy bikinis," as one queen explained. All fundamental differences aside, the crowning process remains similar. For example, once crowned Miss Caldwell Night Rodeo, a girl could then compete for Miss Rodeo Idaho. Since MRI's 1956 inception, most years see over sixty applicants. Perhaps twenty-five make it to the final competition. This year, though, three girls applied. Of the three only one holds a rodeo title. The MRI board, desperate for a competition, told the other two girls if they could come up with sponsorships, they could compete. This year marks an all-time low in contestant applications.[4]

If accepted for the weeklong competition, the queens travel to Nampa, Idaho, where those cowboys cut cattle on the weekends. Nampa requires a twenty-minute drive from Eagle, and it looks like Eagle did thirty years ago. Most people drive pickups. There are still farm fields between subdivisions, and generally people in Eagle avoid Nampa because there are "gangs" and because the sugar beet factory (which sours the Cattlemen's in Caldwell) stinks the whole town up;[5] people in Nampa avoid Eagle because it's crawling with all those damn yuppies. The queens never leave Nampa.

While competing, the queens are not allowed access to any of the following: computers, cell phones, friends, or family.[6] They may not wear their crowns, ever. They will wear the banners provided by the MRI organization. They may ride their own horses in parades but not in competitive events. The queens travel, eat, and sleep together. Historically, drama—of the standard teen-girl variety—has ensued; this year, however, the contestants appear cordial and chatty and friendly. They lend one another lip gloss and help each other pin their banners in place. The perk of a three-girl competition, it seems.

7   I imagine Inkom to be the kind of place that looks like the *New York Times* ad taped to my freezer door. I google the town, and my hunch checks out— meadows and mountains and foothills abound. I envision Abby reading on the porch of her log home, the far-flung prairie her front yard.

8   Wholesome + all-American (?) + moral values + character = ideal?

9   Consider the words Kacey uses—*imagination*, *nostalgia*. Here we have one of the few, perhaps only, suggestions that the cowboy era no longer exists in Idaho. It seems the MRI folks believe Idaho is still defined by a thriving cowboy culture, regardless of its depleted cattle industry, vanishing farm fields, boarded-up slaughterhouses, and quickly sprouting shopping malls (not to mention that MRI itself only had three contestants this year, that ghastly low).

Contestants

Abby Bowler is thin as a rope, with a long, sloping face. A mass of Barbie-blonde hair falls past her shoulders, and she always sports false eyelashes. Abby is from Inkom, Idaho, a town of 206 "families."[7] She wants to be Miss Rodeo Idaho because she is committed to "projecting the image of a wholesome, all-American girl with high moral values and character."[8] Abby speaks with a high, thin voice and seems genuinely, undeniably sweet, though this might be a result of the eyelashes, which she bats masterfully.

Kacey Quibb holds the Meridian Lions Rodeo Queen title and radiates confidence. She speaks loudly with a deep-rasped voice and is clearly a seasoned competitor. She never stops smiling. In fact, she smiles so constantly, it can look pained. She is also always posing—standing heel to toe, hands tucked behind her back—and when she walks, her gait is some strange combination of delicate modeling and graceless strength. She is short and broad and looks really strong. She is solid—straight through the hips and waist—and rippled with muscle. Kacey wants to be Miss Rodeo Idaho because she will, she says, "be a role model for young girls and give them a future filled with hope and desire": "I could help more people understand rodeo and how it can be an exciting event for the family, as it captures the imagination and nostalgia of the cowboy era in America."[9]

Courtney Gilbert is visibly young and visibly nervous. Like the other queens, she is all smiles all the time, but beneath hers lies a hint of undeniable terror. She keeps her hands in her lap, as is advisable, but her fingers never stop dancing. She is a natural, deep blonde and wears less makeup than the other two girls. Courtney stands out for her simple, relatively plain styling. She wears too-bright blush but no foundation, and freckles dapple her nose. She is thin, and her shirts haven't been tailored as carefully as the other girls', and beneath her rhinestones ooze visible clumps of glue. She

10 I learn the best way to cure a horse's biting problem is to bite it back *hard* on the tender, meaty curve of its muzzle.

11 As the queens roll up their sleeves and trace scars, I keep quiet. I've been bucked and nipped, certainly, but I know our war stories are not the same. In a pissing contest, regardless of severity of wound, I lose for this reason: all my injuries were my fault. I raced a hungry Arabian through an alfalfa field, was bucked, and then crashed on the saddle's horn. I broke an arm after jumping a horse saddled in too-long stirrups. I chipped a bone (here the most embarrassing and most recent) after rolling from a still-standing, loose-cinched horse. These girls have seen the same bruises and bangs, but their animals were wild, new to bridles and reins and a spur's stab to the flank.

   Maybe this feeling of inadequacy is more deeply seeded than I'd like to admit. That old boyfriend of mine, the alfalfa farmer, had a sister-in-law who was an ex-queen. She never broke costume: always sporting snug jeans and big buckles and stiff-curled hair. She talked about breaking horses and punching cattle, and I cowered in her presence. Able only to ride trail horses drained of their zest, I felt useless. In the company of the queen, I was a woman impotent in all things "western," as out of place as that barefoot girl on the Boston campus.

12 The girls whisper that Abby packed eighty pairs of carefully painted boots. I can't help but think of my own penchant for boots, though I wear them only for fashion's sake and wouldn't dream of wearing them anywhere near a horse (to be stepped on or stained in manure? the horror!). I splurge on well-crafted, handmade boots: Fryes or Old Gringos. And on this front I had hoped we could talk shop. Of course the queens know all about Ropers and Whites and every other brand, but nice boots don't pertain to queening. That's a different part of their lives—and I'm sure each pair of their boots have stains and spur scratches and probably look all the cooler for it. For competition it's these wear-'em-once, flimsy-heeled numbers, like the boots donned at a Lady Antebellum concert.

is eighteen and claims to be a "cowgirl with many talents!" Court-ney wants to be Miss Rodeo Idaho because, she says, it would be "an honor and one I'm going to work hard for. To be a part of Ida-ho's history and knowing I did many helpful things to help others." She also wants to become a psychologist and hypnotist "because what better way to aid [her] fellow man."

They all tease their hair, which is a given. After the trademark chopping wave, rodeo queens are known more for their enormous barrel curls than anything else. They always, regardless of liberally applied perfume, smell like Aqua Net. They are all from southern Idaho. They all have college aspirations. They have all competed as queens before. They are all supremely kick-ass on a horse. Collec-tively, they barrel race, goat tie, pole bend, and train horses. They are undeniably tough. The queens have been double kicked in the chest, the side, and the back. They have been bucked off and rolled on. They have been bitten. They have bitten horses back.[10] They have punched misbehaving horses straight across the face. They have been flung from the saddle; they have landed hard.[11]

They all wear western attire: hats and Wranglers and handmade blouses dripping in rhinestones. And the outfits always match. For example, on the first day of the competition, Kacey wears robin's-egg blue Wranglers, a matching polyester blouse with a longhorn rhinestoned into the back, and boots spray-painted the same shade of blue. The girls buy cheap boots, five bucks a pop, so they can spray-paint them the exact right hue, and they use car paint because it yields the glossiest sheen.[12] On formal days they wear leather gowns—long-sleeved, high-necked dresses made of oiled and buffed cowhide and dyed in every shade—emerald, eggplant, maroon. Until the 1980s queens were never allowed out of them. The gowns are sold at saddle stores or bought on eBay or handed down from ex-queens. The dresses circulate. Most girls have worn a competitor's gown at some point in time. They are all long-sleeved. They are all tight through the legs. The queens shuffle around in these col-

13 I assume this is because a rodeo queen judge must have (once upon a
   time) been a queen herself, but this is just conjecture.

umns of leather. They are all decorated, usually with rhinestones and scalloped hemlines, though some boast fringe. On the skirt of one of Courtney's dresses, she has embroidered the entire state of Idaho, complete with mountain bluebirds and syringas and spuds. At rodeos they sweat uncontrollably. Comfort is one of the many things the queens sacrifice. Beneath gowns or denim they wear Spanx and panty hose, considerable additions given they circulate rodeo rings in the driest, hottest months. They wrap their feet in grocery bags so they slide more easily into boots. Their scalps are scarred from bobby pins slicing their skin, and the pins are not a cosmetic decision. If a rodeo queen's hat flies off during competition, she is penalized points and fined fifty dollars. The queens bobby pin the hell out of their hats, hitching the band deep into their scalps.

They all hate the big hair.

Judgment

The Categories

The queens are judged in four categories: horsemanship, congeniality, appearance, and personality. All categories are created equal (so says the handbook), but most queening enthusiasts agree horsemanship is the real meat and potatoes. One MRI board member said, "If we got a queen who can't ride, we got a problem." Naturally, others disagree. Some bet it all on appearance. "You don't want a girl representing your state you gotta put a bag on her head, do you?" one MRI enthusiast asked. Another added, "You can teach a girl to ride. Can't teach her to be easy on the eyes." No one talks much about congeniality or personality.

The judges are from Montana and Oregon and Washington. They are farmers or ranchers or horse trainers. They are all women.[13] They are all veteran judges. They wear jackets swaying with fringe or shining with rhinestoned mustangs. They trail the girls

everywhere, writing in notebooks feverishly. In the company of the judges, Abby speaks when spoken to, Courtney talks frantically, never allowing herself enough pause to gain a full breath, and Kacey tucks her hands behind her back and smiles.

In addition to the three judges, there is a team of MRI board members. A clan of ex-queens, in Navajo-inspired print jackets and tight Wranglers, run this show. They get the queens where they need to be, make sure the judges are happy, and deliver food round the clock. They cast no formal vote in choosing the next MRI, but in their company the girls turn it on.

The Events

Everything the queens do is judged. On the first day of the competition, they ride in the Snake River Dayz Parade, where they are judged on appearance, attitude, choice of outfit colors, and how well they interact with parade goers. The MRI organization invites Boise news broadcasters to the competition. How the queens handle the press, judged. They take a written test on the history of rodeo and equine knowledge. This is scored and judged. Each queen submits a headshot. Appearance, expression, and choice of outfit matter, naturally. At any point a judge may ask a queen a question about rodeo trivia or current events. Enunciation, sense of humor, pace of gait, western attire, all judged all the time. The girls never forget they are being watched and scored, not for a second. Abby never leaves her hotel room without her false lashes, Kacey walks through a parking lot as though she is onstage, and Courtney smiles hard.

PERSONAL INTERVIEWS

For the first major event, the queens sit at a round table in a dimly lit conference room in the Idaho Center, home to the Snake River Stampede, a top-ten Professional Rodeo Cowboy Association rodeo. Seating twelve thousand people, this corral ties Boise State University's pavilion for Idaho's largest arena. The girls gather in a con-

14 The girls fire through these questions (impressive, given the sheer bulk of them), and the information is positively foreign to me. But they cover everything: types of ropes and knots, the 1972 Miss Rodeo Idaho's biography, the physiology of the horse. In short the queens sound like historians and Boy Scouts and veterinarians. In short they know their shit.

They say words I've never heard before, whole sentences for which I can't decipher the noun from the verb, and I am in high school again, listening to Ex-Boyfriend's Rodeo Queen Sister-in-Law rattle on about breaking colts, and I feel so unknowing.

ference room aptly, if not uninspiredly, named the Rodeo Room. Abby runs through a four-inch stack of note cards, quizzing Kacey on the varying lengths of spurs and the potential dental problems in brood mares. Kacey knows all the answers. Abby reads half a question, and Kacey rattles off a response. Courtney watches and nods.[14]

Reigning queens mill around the conference room. Once crowned, a queen must attend as many events as possible. Amber Jackson, the 2010 MRI herself, is a tall, thick girl with white-blonde hair. She wears black jeans and boots, and fixed on her hat rests the MRI tiara. The tiara more closely resembles a champion buckle than a crown. It is flat and made of the same heavy silver as a cowboy's belt buckle. It features three intersecting Idahos, carefully lined so that the state's panhandle rises like the prongs of a tiara. Every MRI has worn this crown.

In the corner of the conference room sits a table dedicated to Amber. The photo of Amber among the pines is printed as a poster. Beneath the poster rests a scrapbook of Amber's reign. There are pictures of non-queen Amber with her family—her hair pulled back in a thin ponytail, no cloud of curls here. She wears flared blue jeans and a loose green fleece, a brush of mascara and a thin coat of lip gloss her only makeup. She is plain and pretty and so much younger-looking in these pictures. Throughout the rest of the book, she is back in her queen garb—the sparkling blouses and rainbow-colored jeans and tufts of electrified hair. A photo of Amber with other state queens in an airport looks like some strange sorority picture. Somehow all the girls know to line up and bend at their waists and rest their palms on their knees. But instead of Delta Sigma Theta T-shirts, the queens are a wash of buffed leather and rhinestone-prismed blouses. The book is huge. Photos of Amber posing with rodeo fans. A shot of Amber at the Idaho Potato Museum—a truck-sized ceramic baker glowing behind her. Beside the scrapbook, all the spoils of competition: the MRI saddle, a pair of chaps, heavily fringed; a pair of vintage leather gloves, equally

15 I assume the Bible was opened arbitrarily. Song of Songs seems counter to MRI's insistence on the *ideal* woman—that soap-scrubbed image of a girl (with a rhinestone-encrusted rack and wet, red lips, ironically) who has a cousin, not a boyfriend. All those high morals and good character. But for centuries Hebrew children weren't allowed near Song of Songs for its racy rendering of Solomon and his bride pining for one another. "Honey and milk are under your tongue . . . the roof of your mouth like the best wine." Yowza.

16 One of the queens would buy jeans for all the men in her family.

17 Kacey, speaking deeply and loudly, says she will go on to win Miss Rodeo America and then pursue a career in agriculture. Abby, amid eyelash bats, will be married with two children, named Viv and Gabrielle; and Courtney will hypnotize people. No other explanation offered.

18 Kacey states the problem lies at home—most of Kacey's answers include the words *home* and/or *family*. "It's how they're raised," she says. Courtney, striking a more progressive note, states, "It's up to the individual." The judges look unimpressed, and she adds, "But you can't have your privates hanging out!" Laughter ensues.

19 Abby knocks it out of the park by saying her grandmother's porch because she knows the flag always get respect. Not to be (too) outdone, Kacey prefers a classroom of five-year-olds because seeing pride in children is magical.

20 The answers are all predictable. Courtney and Abby discuss open spaces and fresh air and freedom. Kacey is the only queen to mention Boise—Idaho's "metropolitan" center. She says Idaho is great because you can get a Starbucks in Boise and twenty minutes later be in total wilderness. No one discusses Walmarts or cul-de-sacs, and maybe this is because there are still stretches of Idaho—the stretches these girls call home perhaps—that have yet to see such "progress."

fringed; a photo of the MRI trailer; a mock-check in the amount of twenty-five hundred dollars; a Bible flung open to Song of Solomon.[15] At every turn evidence of Amber's reign.

Amber isn't the only royalty here today. Miss Teen Rodeo Idaho, Paizley Lance, is a tall, shapely sixteen-year-old in aqua-green jeans, shirt, and boots. She is the only honest-to-goodness brunette in the crew. Well, a caveat: Kacey is brunette-ish. She was once a brunette, or still is, but the top layer of her hair is frosted in honey-colored highlights. It seems that going brunette was a good call on Paizley's part. In a roomful of car-painted boots and bedazzled tops, it is difficult to stand out. She, along with Courtney, is one of the few girls who look her age, and she seems the least composed in the bunch. Paizley slouches in her chair and twirls a turquoise ring around her thumb, half-watching the contestants quiz each other. She is relaxed to the point of indifference. She is cool as a cuke. Hadley Sidler sits beside Paizley. The fourteen-year-old Miss Junior Rodeo is tiny waisted and has the only head of hair that might naturally be this voluminous. Uncommonly beautiful, she looks like a middle school Jon Benet with heavily mascaraed eyelashes and deeply painted lips. She does not seem old enough for all that makeup. The two mini-queens talk about their horses, and Paizley tells Hadley the best workout for your legs is riding bareback. "I only ride bareback, and my thighs are solid muscle." Paizley slaps her leg as she says this. Even through denim, the sharp curve of her quadriceps is visible. She is, refreshingly, proud of a little bulk.

The girls go in for their interviews one at a time. The questions range from horse maintenance to rodeo trivia and a host of standard pageant-like questions. How do you handle rejection? If you won the lottery, what would you do?[16] When you're finished queening, what will you do?[17] How would you improve morality in young adults?[18] If you were a flag, where would you fly?[19] Why do you love living in Idaho?[20]

21 I know nothing about horsemanship save the basics. My father, the horse-man in my family, taught me the necessities: how to get where you want to go, what to do if the horse spooks or bucks (spin the horse if you can; try to jump if you can't). Sophistication of this sort is beyond my comprehension. Because of my confessed ignorance, an MRI board member watches the event with me. She is, like most of the people on the board, an ex-queen. Her hair is cropped but still teased at the roots, and she wears lime-green boots with snug jeans and a pink pearl-snap blouse.

22 "First thing to consider," my correspondent tells me, "is that these girls don't get to ride their own horse. Don't even get to see this horse until show time." I nod. "You ride?" she asks me. I tell her I get by, barely (if at all). "So you can appreciate how tall an order that is," she says, and I nod again.

I ask my correspondent if it's dangerous. "Of course. Horses are unpre-dictable animals, and these girls are asking a lot of them." When asked if a girl has ever been hurt, she says, "These girls are good enough to know what to do in a pinch." I remember all my falls from panting trail horses. I remember the stupidly snapped arms, deep-tissue bruises, chipped bones. I wouldn't make it out of that chute.

23 If rodeo queens are known for anything (aside from the hair), it's galloping around rodeo rings at unbelievable speeds, balancing an enormous flag, and waving. The wave is not a relaxed, princessly wave. It is a rigid chop, timed with the horse's rhythm. Every rodeo starts this way. This is the buzz.

24 The lead changes are a big deal. If there is anything my correspondent discusses, it's lead changes. Essentially, when a horse turns, its inside leg should reach farther than the outside. Both front and hind legs must do this. This is accomplished through well-timed taps of the rider's heels and slight shifts in the rider's hips. "It's a lot harder than that sounds," my cor-respondent tells me.

It is not enough to just stop the horse. The queens must make the horse stop on a dime from a full gallop. The horse's legs stiffen straight ahead, and the animal slides through sod, dirt flying. For a moment the queen disappears in a cloud of dust. Catapulting seems imminent, all that veloc-ity unstoppable. It is frightening to watch.

25 Even in MRI's heyday, when nearly ten times this many girls competed, I can't imagine the stands looking any less empty. Maybe one hundred fans instead of twenty. Still a drop in a bucket.

Afterward Kacey sits poised at the table and chats with Amber, her posture erect as ever, her legs crossed at the ankles. When asked how she did, she smiles and nods and says confidently (but not too confidently), "Well." Abby asks Courtney how the interview went, and Courtney says she did okay, she thinks, but there's just never any way to tell, and Abby reassures her.

HORSEMANSHIP

The girls have ten minutes before their next event. They move at this clip all week. The queens rise as early as 3:00 a.m. (it takes at least two hours to get ready in the mornings, and some events, like the Buckaroo Pancake Feed, start at 5:00 a.m.). They shuttle from judged events to convalescent homes to elementary schools, and at night they rehearse their coronation dance till after midnight. Such ass busting seems inhuman.

After the interviews they go downstairs to the rodeo ring for the horsemanship competition.[21] This event requires that each girl memorize three different patterns around the corral. The horses the queens will direct today aren't even trained for this type of riding. They are team rope horses, trained to chase cattle, totally unaccustomed to the sophisticated rein commands the queens will be demanding.[22] They must walk the horse into the corral, mount, execute all the patterns, and then run a buzz.[23] Each pattern requires flying lead changes, spins, stops, and reversals.[24]

The Idaho Center's twelve thousand seats are empty, save a clutter of twenty or so queening fans.[25] The girls sneak waves to their families and head to the chutes to meet the horses. The judges sit behind a rodeo announcer, who, despite the tiny crowd, has all of the Idaho Center's audio system fired up and echoing. The announcer booms portions of Abby's biography, how she's a student at Idaho State University and owns her own stationery company. Abby walks to the center of the ring and mounts. In so doing, she grabs the back panel of the saddle, and a judge tsks. A quick

deduction for sure. Abby runs her patterns and cuts the arena into uneven halves. She struggles for her lead changes and wrestles the horse into reverse. On her final lap she turns and waves at the judges. Her buzz is fast but not too fast, and the flag remains perfectly straight at her hip. Her hair flies behind her, and she is a blur of blonde and sparkle.

Kacey leads her horse from the chute, and the small crowd erupts in applause. One MRI board member, in a moment of undisguised favoritism, claps. Kacey runs her patterns and struggles for a lead change but finally gets it without having to look down or stop the horse. The MRI members whisper about the lead changes and the flying stops and the way Kacey sits in the saddle. They call Kacey "Kace." The members clap and say she made a few mistakes—could have mounted a little more cleanly, could have gotten the lead changes more quickly—but "she got there."

Courtney mounts, and like Abby and Kacey, she grabs the back of the saddle. Such an easy mistake, everyone is surprised. Courtney lopes around the arena and bounces from her saddle. "She's used to riding Arabians," one MRI member says. "They travel differently." On the quarter horse Courtney springs from the horse's back. Other than her sloppy positioning, her ride is the strongest. From the stands Courtney's nervous smile isn't visible. The horse spins when she pulls it to spin; the horse leads with the left when Courtney taps her heel. She shifts from lope to trot to gallop at all the right times. She yanks the reins, and the horse flies to a stop. She doesn't hesitate for a moment, and the horse obeys. She is nothing but confidence. Courtney finishes her ride and dismounts and leads the horse to the chute. "She didn't turn to the judges," one observer points out. "She had a good ride. Kept coming out of that saddle but a good ride."

An MRI chaperone takes the girls from the chutes directly to a van, and they can only wave again at their families as they leave.

26 I eat on the other side of the room at a table full of ex-queens and their mothers. At some point each ex-queen casually mentions how many titles she holds. A large-boned woman who towers beside me trumps them all with nine.

Courtney and Kacey chat as they cross the parking lot, relaxed and happy with their rides, and Abby is quiet.

In the parking lot the MRI members place bets. Most everyone agrees this category will come down to Kacey or Courtney, but in general they are impressed with each ride. All three are clearly good horsewomen. They were all poised and in control and rode along with a relaxed athleticism. "At least we'll have a girl who can ride, regardless," a board member says.

SPEECHES

The queens scurry into the New Meadows Golf Course Lodge, where there will be an open-to-the-public luncheon and the contestants will give a speech. For said public—namely families and friends of the girls and queening diehards, typically meaning ex-queens and their mothers—the cost of the Salisbury steak and scalloped potatoes lunch is twelve dollars. The queens are in their formal garb today. No more jeans and bedazzled blouses. Nothing but head-to-toe leather gowns and fresh white hats. The dresses groan as they move. They smell like new cars. Abby wears a teal gown with a mermaid hemline; Kacey is in deep-purple Supersuede with ragged lines of gold glitter; and Courtney wears her tan, fringed Idaho gown—this the dress that pays homage to the Gem State: the embroidered silhouette and leaping trout, the chirping bluebirds, their song marked by quarter notes sewn above their beaks. When it's time, they go through the buffet and sneak away to say hello to their mothers, somewhere in line behind them. After a quick, clandestine hug, the queens shuffle to their table and sit together.[26]

When asked if they are nervous, Kacey, with zero hesitation, says, "We've just done this so many times. It's really no big deal anymore." The banquet room is full. About fifty people salt their steaks and wait to hear from the girls. Delivering a speech to a room full of ex-competitors could be daunting, but the girls chat and clean their plates. On the stage the MRI banner is raised and tacked.

27 Interesting that the slogan specifies *our* western way of life. Maybe this is an open acknowledgment of the modulations in Idaho's identity. This is the Idaho of split-rail fences and worn-soft saddles, not the Idaho of denim boutiques and cupcake shops. And maybe this suggests that the MRI folks realize few Idahoans buck and bronc anymore, and maybe they just don't care. This is *their* Idaho, and it's the only one worth promoting, they seem to say.

28 I am all for spreading the love, to be sure. But the phrase *our western way of life* is repeated by all the queens and board members so frequently that I continue to question what exactly the queens are promoting. And though I wonder if when they say "our" way of life, they literally mean to suggest the lives of rural, non–Treasure Valley Idahoans, no one ever says so directly, and so I can't be sure. What's more, didn't this ex-queen just explain it's a love for *the* western way of life? And so I'm left to ask: What does the western life look like? This year's contestants are all from rural, southern Idaho, and when they say "western," they summon the archetype of this place: Top 40 country blaring from barn stalls; kids shucking corn on front porches; girls in pretty pink blouses; girls wrestling horses into submission. And for them this is Idaho; this is the West. But this portrayal does not encompass all of Idaho, and it is does not wholly encapsulate what it means to be western. It is, more aptly, an idea of the West, a version of this place, and it is one these women think deserves promoting.

Perhaps what is most compelling is the idea that it *needs* promoting. If we allow Idaho to be signified only by its Old West heritage (spurs, prairies, buckin' broncs), then surely that Idaho is endangered. As we know, only three women applied to be MRI this year, and only southern Idaho is represented. Historically, the applicants have come from Nampa and Eagle and Boise—not just the agricultural communities of the high desert. Now, though, queening is only represented by the country girls from way out in the sticks, Inkom and Pocatello and Blackfoot.

29 The ex-queen raises a worthy point. If Miss Rodeo Idaho, that ideal western woman, serves as an ambassador for the sport of rodeo, then what are we to make of the opportunities available for her in this sport? There are seven standard rodeo events: men wrestle steer, men team rope, men tie-down rope, men ride saddle bronc, men ride bareback, and men ride bulls. Women barrel race. And if a woman can't barrel race or doesn't enjoy barrel racing, there is no room for her in the actual sport as a competitor. But she can tease her hair and bedazzle a dress and pin a glittered banner to her chest.

30 Miss Rodeo America is the Big One, worth the whole kit and caboodle. Each December, at the National Rodeo Finals (held in Las Vegas, sort of strangely), the country's best bronc riders and barrel racers compete andMiss Rodeo America is crowned. Idaho, tied with California, holds the most MRA titles—a statistic worthy of any Idahoan's pride,

On it the logo: a silhouette of the state of Idaho buckled beneath a spur. To the right the slogan: "Royally Promoting Our Western Way of Life."[27] An ex-queen explains that this is what queening is all about. "It's about a love for the western way of life," she repeats. "It's a way of spreading that love."[28] She continues, "Plus, if you don't barrel race, there isn't a whole lot you can do to be part of the rodeo. If you want to be involved, you got to queen."[29]

After the carrot cake, the pageant coordinator, a tiny, round-faced woman with enormous eyes and broad, full lips, introduces Amber. "Amber's done a wonderful job for us this year," the coordinator says. "And she's had to learn so many new things. Like packing for the airport. She has some wonderful stories." The petite brunette hands the mic to Amber. "I travel with twenty-eight queens, and we all have the same goal: to be Miss Rodeo America.[30] And I just love getting to know their aspects on it." Amber continues, "And I've met so many neat people on the airplanes. It's amazing what conversations come up when you're dressed as a rodeo queen on a plane where nobody knows anything about rodeo. I've been asked so many rules, like how long *does* a cow have to stay down in tie-down roping?" Amber's speech reiterates the purpose of the rodeo queen: to be an ambassador for the sport, to raise awareness and appreciation for rodeo, and to, as the banner promises, represent the (a?) western way of life.

As Amber finishes, Courtney and Abby are escorted out to the hall. No other contestants may be in the room while a queen gives her speech. Once the girls leave, Kacey walks toward the stage. A member of the Meridian Lions Club escorts Kacey through the crowd, though perhaps it is more accurate to say Kacey pulls him there. She blazes for the stage, and the man clings to her elbow. Once she gets to the microphone stand, Amber introduces her, and the room clatters with applause and clearing dishes.

Kacey bows her head and then, in a burst of theatrical flair, flashes up her right hand. "Rigid and wild," her hand waves in half-circles given that our beauty queen analogue, Miss Idaho, has never won (or even come *close* to winning) Miss America. These queens get it done.

31 Kacey delivers her speech in a start-stop rhythm. She stutters through her sentences but not because she is unprepared or stammering; her mid-clause pauses are stylistic.

32 I recognize this line from a Jeff Foxworthy bit. It's his joke word for word, and if I notice the line, then the judges (who seem like bigger Foxworthy fans than I) probably notice it too. But this small plagiarism doesn't seem to bother anyone.

as she speaks. "Adventure and passion, a leader in technology that storms into [*pause*] the twenty-first century.[31] Here we have [*pause*] Idaho," she nearly whispers the state's name. Then, with immediate energy, "Many clever comments are made about our trademark [*pause*] taters and spuds [*big energy on the word* spuds], but it's our dairies and cattle ranches that are the [*pause, air quotes*] cash cow that drive Idaho's economy." Kacey speaks with an enthusiasm that will go unmatched. "Sacajawea was born a member of the Shoshone tribe but was captured as a young child. She made her way home as the guide and beacon for the Lewis and Clark expedition." The pause here, at the end of the sentence, feels natural. Kacey plants a hand on her hip and says, "You can take a girl out of Idaho, but you can't take Idaho out of the girl!" She finishes, "From world-class resorts to small cozy towns, Idaho will reel you in [*gestures reeling*] like a shimmering rainbow trout [*half-circles with hands*]. Here we have Idaho, winning her way to fame. Esta perpetua, may she live forever."

The crowd erupts. The judges jot notes and nod in pleased approval. Kacey stands in her careful, heel-toe stance and smiles graciously.

Kacey leaves, and Courtney enters. Like the horsemanship competition, Courtney is less nervous performing than she is in the presence of the other competitors. As Amber introduces her, she paces the stage, stopping in front of the judges, posing with her hand on her hip and spinning. She walks to the microphone and begins, "Clear skies, fresh crystal-clear water, wild deer not more than one hundred feet away from you? Mountains surrounding a tiny valley? Do you know where you can find all this? I can find that in the great state of Idaho." Courtney speaks easily, slowly. "Idaho has four seasons: winter, almost winter, still winter, and construction."[32] Her comedic timing is spot-on, and the judges laugh with her. "Maybe that's what makes us cowboys and cowgirls so tough?" Though she flexes a bicep and winks at the judges with an off-the-

33 I assume Courtney is referring to Idaho's rather paltry population—just over one million people, nailing it in the top ten least-populated states in America, though it's the fourteenth largest state, area wise. (All this space! So few people! That old story rears its head again.)

34 This, too, is a Foxworthy joke from the same routine, and it's bizarre that two girls would hijack cracks from the same comedian. Maybe these speeches are as shared as the queens' gowns—passed around, inherited?

charts campiness, she poses the question with a chatty ease. "Idaho may be a small state, but its people hold it high in their hearts," and with this nicely articulated sentiment, Courtney lowers the microphone and allows applause.[33]

Abby forgoes the cross-stage modeling and walks directly to the podium. As Amber reads her introduction, she shifts uneasily, smoothing her hands along her waist and hips. Abby's dress is clearly the most expensive, made of buffed, supple leather, and her rhinestones, clear as diamonds, have been seamlessly fastened to the gown. The other queens murmur it cost three thousand dollars. Naturally, it has been nicely tailored, but even still it is too large in the waist. This is no failing of the gown, as no seamstress would be able to curve a seam so drastically. Abby's stomach is unfeasibly narrow. The dress sags across her. She flips tufts of hair over her left shoulder, then her right. Cameras flash, and she remembers to smile. Abby starts quietly, "Idaho: A diamond in the rough. Majestic northern Idaho: lakes and forest. Vibrant southwestern Idaho: rivers and canyons." It is clear she has chosen these words carefully, that she is striving for a poeticism the other girls neglected. "Idaho is a big state," she continues. "This place offers more than just potatoes. Did you know Idaho companies sold goods and services to more than 144 countries?" Her voice becomes louder, more enthused. "So much for [air quotes] small potatoes. But what makes Idaho really great? We do of, course." Here she relaxes a bit. She stares directly at the judges and whispers, "Shh [places finger on lips], I don't like to tell many people, but this is why I pride myself in saying that I am from Idaho!" She nearly shouts Idaho, then immediately shifts into a gentler register. "It is the gentleman who opens the door for me at the post office. The mother in the minivan who slows to let me into traffic when I'm driving into town. A place where you can have a five-minute conversation with someone who dialed the wrong number [knowing laughter from audience].[34] A place where you can be trailing cows and your elementary school princi-

35 All of the queens' speeches dwell on the same details, careful to include MRI history and rodeo trivia. They each discuss Idaho geography and industry, and the rhetoric of their speeches, the visuals they offer, partake in the *idyllic* portrayal of this place: mountains and rivers and soft-eyed deer; principals in church clothes capturing bulls; polite, minivan-driving mothers; Bible believers; kindly country folk. And the landscape is nothing but wild rivers and tremendous mountains. No queen discusses strip malls or movieplexes or subdivisions. Nothing about Eagle's themed living communities. Nothing about the miles of flat, color-leached desert. No one describes the Treasure Valley, its traffic-jammed freeways and Walmarts and cul-de-sacs. And though these girls are indeed from rural Idaho, where perhaps the mythic story of this place rings true-ish, over half of Idaho's population, as they have likely studied, lives in the Treasure Valley. Though the queens do not call the Treasure Valley home, they surely know it exists. They have spent a week in Nampa, and they see that this place isn't just rogue bulls and deep canyons. But the tract houses of Nampa and the coffee shops and bistros of Eagle (so unromantic) are not the Idaho these queens are promoting. There is no room for that Idaho here.

36 Perhaps family dinners weren't at the top of the founding fathers' agenda, but Kacey's careful preparation is, as usual, undeniable. She has successfully mentioned the home, family values, and the ideals that built this great nation. The judges scribble notes giddily.

37 This rare moment of collective jitters sends my stomach into knots. The girls have been more than accommodating, happy to explain tie-down roping or share their most horrific queening faux pas (which, as promised, shall remain off-the-record). I hold my breath as each queen answers.

pal stops, in his church clothes, to help get a rogue bull trotting off into someone's nice green lawn. Idaho is a true gem." As Abby finishes, a polite smattering of applause rises from the lunchers, and she turns immediately to Amber and hands off the microphone. Before leaving the stage, she stands, heel to toe, and turns, smiling in the flash of firing cameras, the queen on display.[35]

The queens' speeches were carefully planned and smoothly delivered. No one stammered or forgot their lines. But the girls are not through. Now Amber will ask each of them two questions. At this portion each of them becomes nervous. They swallow or lick their lips before answering. First, she wants to know what the queens would do to help curb childhood obesity. Kacey's answer begins with "I believe that childhood obesity occurs right at the home level," and she goes on to say, "It's important to keep those high values that the U.S. was founded on, and that's having a great home-cooked meal."[36] Abby talks about jogging with her horse Trigger, and Courtney takes an unwelcome, progressive approach. "Show them the nutrition facts, and they won't gain weight if that's their issue," she says. "And they can still look beautiful. You can go out and find a person who might be overweight, and they think they're beautiful. Bring those people in and show them how great they can be, and they can shine. They don't need to worry about their weight," she finishes. The crowd applauds tentatively, politely, for this response.

Next Amber asks the queens what has most impressed them in their lifetime. At this question, each queen falters. Surely the queens studied current events and Idaho history. This question, though, seems amorphous, vague, personal. Even Kacey needs a minute. Each of them stammers.[37] Kacey replies, "The person I've become," and Abby, in a similar vein, says she is impressed that she has "learned so much about rodeo, all by myself." Courtney says, with undeniable charm, "I'm surprised I'm still a cowgirl! I'm serious. I've been bucked off so many times, you'd think I'd walk

38 I assume they are referencing the "I'm most impressed with myself" moment, which was no crowd-pleaser.

away from it." Courtney's answer is sincere and believable. The youngest and most unsteady queen has handled this question as though there were no judges, no scorepads, no crowd of belching luncheon goers sizing up her every word. The judges smile, and after the obesity slipup, Courtney has recovered.

At the end of the luncheon my correspondent from the horsemanship competition whispers with other MRI board members. It's close, they say. Kacey, though composed, lacked the poeticism of Abby, and at times she seemed a bit overconfident.[38] Plus Abby seems sweet as a bug and that voice so delicate, but her ride, alas, wasn't the strongest. And Courtney's charm, though undeniable, can be unbridled; she can be too informal. And when she isn't onstage or performing, when it is just her and the girls and the judges, she is jittery with nerves, fueled by a novice's adrenaline. This will be a close one.

Coronation

At the end of the week, the MRI folks invite the community to join them for a coronation event. It is scheduled to take an hour, and they have arranged for a pair of morning radio hosts to emcee. The coronation is not merely a party where the new MRI is announced. A few competitions remain, and the girls cannot yet rest easy.

The show begins without the queens. The MRI board members have put together an Old West skit—Nampa's police chief plays a hell-raising drunk, and the gun he waves, the queens are sure, is real; an ex–rodeo queen is a madam, and the Nampa Civic Center's stage masquerades as an old saloon. The skit buys time for the girls to prep. The coronation requires wardrobe changes. First, a dancing outfit, then each queen will model her finest gown.

The dressing room is a closet washed in dim yellow lights. The walls are cinder blocks painted the color of brown mustard. A counter stretches along the wall, and light bulbs frame the mirror, a stab at green room glamour. The reigning queens, Amber and

39 I imagine this is from nerves. All week each girl has cleaned her plate: pizza and sub sandwiches and rubber chicken dinners. No lettuce picking here. Plus, as the coronation marches on, they will send me to raid the Civic Centers' kitchen. I will bring a platter loaded with rolls and cheese and chocolate cake, and it will be cleaned in minutes.

40 Chukars are fat, striped birds similar to pheasants. Too fat to fly quickly and notoriously stupid, they make easy targets. Idahoans shoot 'em up with real vigor.

41 In truth this does not surprise me. Though I do not keep a gun, my sister packs. By proxy the queens might approve.

Hadley and Paizley, are back for the final day. Each queen has a chair in front of the mirror and a vase full of chocolates. The reigning queens keep a candy in their mouth always. They chat and roll Hershey's Kisses from one cheek to the other. The competitors don't touch their jars.[39] Instead, they bend at their waists and whip their hair so it dangles to the ground. They mist hairspray until the air becomes hazardous. Lips stick with residual Aqua Net. They blot lipstick and rub rouge into their cheekbones. Courtney chats with Hadley and Paizley; Kacey asks Amber about her reign; Abby listens to her iPod. The MRI president, a woman with a feathered mullet and a nametag (in the shape of a sheriff's star) that reads PRESIDENT, checks in on the girls. She walks straight to Hadley, the tiny fourteen-year-old Miss Junior Rodeo Idaho, and cups her chin. "That mascara's still smudged," she says. Hadley jerks away and rolls her eyes. It becomes obvious, for the first time, that Hadley's mother is the president of MRI.

The president pulls up a seat and asks how the girls are doing, and they all nod and smile and say fine, just fine. In minutes, with the most natural of segues, the queens discuss their weapons. "My sister," Amber offers, "was eight months pregnant when some guy knocked on her door late at night. Her husband was out chukar hunting or something, and she thought it was a murderer.[40] So she opened that door with a rifle pointing straight out. Eight months pregnant!" The queens laugh. Then Amber says it's high time she get around to packin', and the president tells her, "If you're gonna get a concealed weapon, get it through Utah because Utah is recognized all throughout the West. A Utah permit is good in Oregon or Idaho or Nevada. Everyone recognizes Utah. That's why I can pack anywhere I go." All these ex-queens, women in ass-tight denim and teased hair and frosty pink lips, likely have .22s strapped beneath those leather-fringed jackets.[41]

A walkie-talkie at the president's hip crackles, and she jets out the door, yelling, "Go time, ladies!" The girls leap to action. They

42 Mutton bustin' is a rodeo-er's first event. Toddlers straddle sheep and try to hang tight as the sheep lopes to the far end of the corral. It is adorable and terrifying. Those who ride well leap and squeal in the center ring. The others, who are trampled or bucked, limp away crying or are carried to an ambulance.

straighten hats and lean into the mirror. They reapply lipstick and sprits petunia body spray into their pits.

Dancing

After the opening skit, the lights die, and the queens get into formation backstage. A Wrangler commercial projects against the stage's red curtain. "Long live cowboys!" shouts a round-faced mutton buster.[42] "Long live cowboys," says a bull rider, fixed in his chute. "Long live cowboys!" yells a perky girl perched on a hay bale. The commercial closes, and Amber bursts through the curtains. In the spotlight, with her white hair and white hat and millions of rhinestones, she shines. "Hey!" she yells, "What about us cowgirls!?"

And with that all the queens—the competitors and reigning royalty—take the stage. They wear matching black Wranglers and black T-shirts with the words GO AHEAD, HOTSHOT! running across a cowgirl pointing a rifle. Pink bandanas dangle from their necks, and everyone but Amber wears a black hat. Amber wears white and that buckle crown. The song, "Thank God I'm a Country Girl" cues, and all the girls shimmy their hips a little as Amber twirls and kicks her way through a solo. This is the format for the whole three-minute performance. All the queens shake their rears lightly as one queen dances a solo and introduces herself. The solo usually involves one slow spin, a firing of imaginary six-shooters, and a flip of the hair, in some unique arrangement.

Each introduction begins with name, title or sponsor, hometown, and name of parents. The insistence on place and family remains a constant. Kacey nails all her moves, her Vaselined teeth shining in the hard light. Courtney shakes with a relaxed, bona fide rhythm, and Abby, who has been concerned about the dance portion all week, doesn't forget a step but moves awkwardly. She is, it's clear for the first time, knock-kneed, and each swirl of her hips is rigid and disjointed. As she traverses the stage, she becomes pigeon-toed. At the end of the song, the queens coagulate at the center

of the stage. Amber stands in the middle, her arms raised in the spotlight. Courtney kneels in the front; Abby and Hadley bend at Amber's feet, their hands on their knees, their small bottoms jutting behind them; brunette Paizley, who has three inches on everyone, looms beside Amber; and Kacey stands beside the reigning queen, her face half-lit in the light. "Thank God I'm a Country Girl!" they yell in unison. The spotlight dies, and the crowd's applause buries the deep shuffle of boots leaving the stage.

Modeling

After the dance number, the queens rush offstage to the changing room. The show started late, and the opening skit went longer than anticipated, and now the queens are behind schedule. The Civic Center is a quarter-full with maybe fifty people, and their lunch hours are ending. The crowd thins. Once in the green room, the girls *move*. Hatboxes fly open and crash to the ground. Queens tear their banners from their T-shirts and sweep their hair up as a competitor pins their sash to their gown. The clatter of tossed belt buckles and zipping leather. The president reenters, clipboard pressed to her chest, and yells, "Hustle, hustle," and the queens obey. They change earrings and respray their hair and pull on new boots.

None of the girls seems nervous about modeling. They are too rushed for nerves. While modeling, the girls must reintroduce themselves and list their scholastic achievements and ambitions. They are judged on personality and appearance, naturally, but creativity and flair are also considered. Presentation, confidence, and stage presence are also judged. With no visible nerves, the girls line up next to the stage and wait their turn.

One of the emcees says, "Not only can they get dirty in the ring, but they can then turn around with the poise and grace required of a rodeo queen." At *queen* Amber strolls onto the stage. Her gown is forest-green, and the fringe starts at her hips and drapes all the way to her boots. With each step, a swish. Amber circles the stage

43 I assume this song was written for the MRI institution. I have never heard it till now, and according to the internet, it doesn't exist. Interesting, though, that the song's refrain includes *still*, as though it is strange to be a cowgirl in Idaho in 2011.

Of course, it is strange, sort of. Half of Idaho's population rests in the undeniably suburban Treasure Valley, and even those small ranching communities are losing pasture to housing tracts. Though they are proud to still be cowgirls and only three girls applied for competition, no one ever openly acknowledges that Idaho is no longer dominated by rural living. Here I see the same blindness to change I found in those cutting horse corrals. These folks pretend Idaho is a land of cattle and cowgirls. Perhaps when they say promote, they mean preserve.

from end to end and back again. She stops stage left, stage right, poses with her hands on her hips, then walks to the center and smiles at the judges, that fringe still swinging. As she paces, the song "Still an Idaho Cowgirl" blares from the PC.[43] Amber's modeling is simple, subdued, more of a stroll than a catwalk stomp, but her shoulders are pulled back, and her smile is visible from the back row. Our queen pacing, we all look on.

Again, men chaperone the girls to the stage. The MRI president's husband holds the girls' hands and takes them to the steps. Abby models first. Her gown, the same luxuriously deep-buffed leather she has worn all week, is glossy black with a slight flare in the skirt and a burst of rhinestones at the waist. Against the black dress her frosted curls shine. Her rhinestones shoot prisms. Strange that after her awkward dance routine, her model walk is all hip swivels. She swings her arms and rolls her hips. She's got energy and sass and a tinge of sex appeal. She circles the stage in a million mini-rotations, and then, standing before the judges, she pops out her hip and switches her feet backward—a half-speed running man, like Hammer on downers. The crowd erupts. Flair, creativity, check, check.

As soon as Kacey hits the stage, she poses. She stands like a beauty queen in a swimsuit, legs carefully tucked, hands placed behind her back, and allows the audience to eye her. Then she walks. Kacey does not move with the same grace as Abby, and she wears a tight-through-the-legs, restrictive gown. Once at center stage, Kacey begins boldly with a quick, heel-kicked spin. She takes mini-steps toward the judges, leans forward, and smiles, though the smile is so eager it appears she is merely offering her teeth for inspection. She storms around the stage in figure eights. Kacey shuffle-stomps to the mic and, for once, flounders. Her voice catches in her throat as she says, "I aspire to go on to . . . a degree . . . a in master's degree or law school depending on what I decide to go on to." She makes her way back to the center of the stage and twirls three times; she keeps spinning till she is offstage, like an ice skater with no ice.

44 That Courtney, in the biggest moments of the competition, wears polyester seems strange. In the queens' absence, the MRI members whisper. The night before the coronation, Kacey and Abby received flowers from their parents. Their mothers handed off good luck baskets to the MRI president to give to their daughters. Abby wears the finest gowns, and anytime Kacey goes near a stage, half the crowd loses it. Courtney's makeup is usually plain, her clothes simple. "Courtney's parents don't seem to really get queening," one member says. They are considering setting aside a small fund for girls who don't receive flowers next year. "Plain heartbreaking," says the president.

45 For nearly an hour I have watched women twirl onstage, whipping their hair, shining in a spotlight. I google "Lady Antebellum's Hillary Scott" to see if somewhere in her Nashville childhood she competed as a rodeo queen. I find nothing, but their shared stiff shoulder wiggles and hard smiles seem to transcend coincidence.

Courtney's gown is not leather.[44] She wears a polyester two-piece ensemble the color of eggshells with a white hat and boots. Once Courtney steps onstage, one person lets out a low whistle. Courtney does not model for as long as the other girls. She does not use the whole stage. She circles a few times before the judges, then takes the microphone and says, "Hi, I'm Courtney." It sounds like a voice-mail recording, a chatty, long drawl on *hi*. "I plan to go to ISU in the fall, where I will study psychology. Then I'll become a hypnotist to help people break their habits or overcome their temptations." A few chuckles from the crowd are hidden beneath modest applause. Courtney spins a few more times, and then, without the taut shoulders and long strides of a model, she walks offstage.[45]

Questions

After the modeling portion, there is a final hurdle—one more interview. Beneath the glowing spotlight and pounds of foundation, with hairspray-filmed cheeks and sweat pooling in their boots, each queen must once more wow the judges. A judge will ask each girl this question: "What do you find are the most difficult decisions to make?" And each girl, having never before heard this question, must push herself to stand with abs flexed, chest up, arms back, and answer.

Kacey takes the stage first. Not surprisingly, she offers a nicely practiced, clean answer about following your heart. Abby speaks to the importance of seeking the counsel of others, and Courtney forges into unexpected territory. "The most difficult decisions that are hard to make," she begins, "are when you have two different sides you want to please. On one side your dad might say, 'Don't eat the peanut butter.' On the other your mom says, 'Eat the peanut butter! You need your strength.' So which parent do you obey?" Somehow, though her response is less conventional than the other girls' and she never really expounds, her charm carries her. And when in doubt, mentioning pleasing your parents seems like a wise

46 The queens talk about champ bull riders like they are heartthrob movie stars, and here we are of one accord. The appeal of the rugged rodeo-er is not lost on me (recall my sorrow over Idaho's diminished cattle industry, how bummed I am that the cowboy has nearly died out), but part of my crush may have to do with the cowboy's mystery. I have no clue how to wrestle a steer. I don't know anything about tying a lariat or tossing a lasso. It's the cowboy's exoticism (combined with his toughness, admittedly) that keeps me so attracted. But these queens know all about roping and tying and riding. In this way, then, perhaps they want to not only bed the cowboy but to be him as well. Perhaps the pageant itself—one of the only inroads rodeo offers women—reflects this two-pronged desire?

move. The crowd clearly likes it, and Courtney comes off as sweet and well intentioned, and she has, effectively but subtly, channeled the importance of kindness and family in one fell swoop. The audience laughs and claps, and Courtney strides across the stage.

Passing the Crown

After the final interview, a tangle of MRI board members huddles in the hall. The judges deliberate in a back room, filling out final evaluations, and the MRI board can only speculate. Everyone is confident Courtney will take home horsemanship, and Abby will likely win the appearance categories, and Kacey interviewed so well. But who will take the tiara, no one can guess.

An accountant has been hired to tally the judges' votes. Everyone waits on the results. Onstage the MRI president and pageant coordinator thank their sponsors. Amber talks more about her adventures as Miss Rodeo Idaho—trips to Florida, Disney World, meeting champion bull riders and blushing in their presence.[46] The crowd has nearly vanished. The coronation has lasted almost three hours. Only the parents remain.

As the pageant winds down onstage, the queens slouch in the green room. There is nothing to do but wait, and where one would expect shaking legs and nervous chitchat, there is only exhaustion. The queens pick at stale rolls. They peel open their chocolates. Abby listens to her iPod, and Courtney rests her eyes. Kacey uses a flyer with her photo on it as a fan. Eventually, as the time to retake the stage nears, they re-powder their noses, re-blast their curls. Plumb exhaustion has worn away all decorum, and they are relaxed, natural. No more eye bats from Abby or square shoulders from Kacey or mile-a-minute jabber from Courtney. Kacey gases the room with hairspray and admits to fantasizing about lopping off her hair. Every queen cops to harboring such visions. They bemoan the early mornings. Amber says there's been a million times this year she wished she could've passed the crown. "Ten months of travel. No breaks,"

47 Maybe this is because Hadley has remained nearly silent through the whole competition or because her feelings about queening, either good or bad, have never been voiced or because everyone realizes that with her mother as president, there's no way she won't be in the ring in three years.

That is, if there are enough girls for a competition in three years. All this talk of future competitions seems to ignore the fact that this year the pageant's pulse is a murmur, a gasping thirty beats per minute. MRI's endangered status remains tacit.

While the queens are working to promote (preserve?) their vision of the West, it occurs to me that they could use a little promotion and preservation themselves. If the trend continues, MRI will vanish—like the mint field, the slaughterhouse—in no time at all. MRI will be another cycle of death or (more optimistically) another opportunity for evolution. But where would Courtney or Abby or even, with all her chutzpah and confidence, Kacey go? To the openly abhorred beauty queen world? I doubt they'd resort to that, and even if they did, I'm worried about how well they might compete. If Lady A can't cut it as just a pop act, then can these girls make it as just beauty queens? And would we want such a thing? To lose all the athleticism and physical rigor and knowledge of Idaho history and industry that goes along with nabbing the buckle crown seems a shame. And let us remember MRI's purpose: to support rodeo, which still thrives in Idaho. The Snake River Stampede is always a sold-out show, the huge arena filled with suburbanites and hipsters and rednecks alike. And so the rodeo world is alive and well; it's just the queen we fear for. Demand persists, but supply is the tricky part. And what if girls stop showing up for competition? What if the Snake River Stampede does without its reigning lady? To allow this partial death, to let rodeos evolve without the queen, is to allow the sport to become even more male dominated. Or maybe if we allow room for evolution, the whole sport might turn on its head. Women might take to bronc riding or bull riding or cattle tying. The possibilities could be endless.

she says. "But you just gotta buck up," she concludes with corn-fed resolve. Paizley agrees queening can be a real pain, but she's had more interview experience and public speaking practice than any other seventeen-year-old she knows. "Anything will be easy after this," she says, and all the queens nod in agreement. Hadley, who still hasn't fixed her smudged mascara, texts and ignores the chatter.

Then Amber asks each girl to try on the crown. "So when it's time, I know which notch to set it to." Courtney is notch three, Abby notch three, and Kacey four. Amber asks Kacey twice which notch. Except for Courtney, all the contestants agree that they will not try again next year. "This is it," Kacey says. "I've got a degree, and I want to work." Abby offers no explanation but says that she will not be back. Paizley, who will be eighteen next summer, says she'll try, and nobody asks Hadley.[47] Usually Amber doesn't like to think about giving up the crown, she says. "Been doing it my whole life, after all." The mood of the room has shifted. Exhaustion and nerves have stripped away all pageantry. When asked why they decided to compete, Abby and Courtney say for the experience, for the traveling opportunities, for the scholarship money. Kacey does not answer right away. She waits, collects her thoughts, and says, with loads of pragmatism, that it's a good networking opportunity. Then, with less polish, remembering that the votes have been cast and the judges aren't near, she says earnestly that queening is what she loves best. The horses and late-summer nights and hours spent in the corral, there is nothing else she'd rather do—and for the first time all week, Kacey looks vulnerable. Then no one speaks, and Hadley peels open a Twix bar, and Paizley sighs, and Amber asks if anybody knows where a fan might be.

Minutes before the girls take the stage, a woman in dusted Wranglers and a boxy gray T-shirt walks into the green room. Behind her follows a round-faced, five-year-old missing a front tooth. She wears teeny black leather chaps and shining purple boots and a shirt made of tinfoil-esque, silver polyester. Her face is framed in a

48 Riley does not look pleased or displeased with all this attention. She is smiling but not in the relaxed, genuine way of children. She is here on business, she realizes. And her mother realizes this too. "You can keep right on taking her picture," she tells me, unhappy with the too-wide positioning of her legs in my first photo. "Oh no, I hate to make her keep posing," I say. "She'll stay like that all day. Won't move one bit. Watch." I see that the mother is intent, so I raise my camera again, and sure enough, Riley doesn't move or blink or breathe. Her smile doesn't crack.

49 I can't help but imagine thirteen years from now, a heavy-chested, glittered-out Riley posing alone on the stage, the star of a one-girl pageant.

50 I am nervous for each of them. After a week of shadowing, I am invested. I've fetched sodas and lugged hatboxes. I've pinned sashes to waists and changed buckles onto fresh belts. I have watched each girl flounder onstage. I have watched each girl muster amazing energy, perseverance, and charm. I have learned about horse breaking and Idaho history and nail polish. I have watched them closely enough to realize that though they each stand poised, each is nervous. Kacey's smile borders on psychotic. Courtney keeps closing and opening her mouth. Every so often Abby shakes her hair softly.

legion of spirals. Fixed to her hat, a cardboard Idaho spray-painted gold. MRI 2023 is Magic Markered across the homemade crown. At the little girl's entrance, all the queens perk up. "Riley!" Courtney squeals. Abby hugs her, and Kacey offers her candy, and Paizley tells her she likes her crown. Riley's belt buckle reads MISS IDAHO PONY CLUB RODEO QUEEN. She rode in the Snake River Dayz Parade with the queens earlier in the week, and she is here to wish the girls good luck. She poses for pictures, both her hands at her sides, one leg kicked before her. Kacey holds up a hand and says, "Hang on!" She kneels and positions Riley's front legs closer together, heel to toe. "Like that," she says, and Riley keeps smiling.[48]

The accountant is double-checking his work, and the girls head to the stage with Riley in tow. The emcees wave Riley into the spotlight. She stands, poised and silent. The radio hosts yell, "Welcome our MRI 2023!" and the crowd *awws* and claps, and the queens join her onstage for a photo op.[49] Behind the curtain Riley's mother beams.

Riley scoots backstage, and the queens follow her. The radio hosts announce the prizes: the horse trailer, the twenty-five-hundred-dollar scholarship, the chance at the Miss Rodeo America crown. Then they welcome the girls back onto the stage, and Courtney takes the lead, then Abby, then Kacey. They stand huddled in the center light.[50] With no more delay, the radio hosts say the winner of the Most Photogenic award will take home an eight-by-ten-inch picture frame and a silver necklace. Kacey's name is called, and she takes a half-step forward and waves. The other girls smile on impeccably. The scrapbook award goes to Abby Bowler, and Abby steps forward, her skirt sparkling in the light, and waves. "Miss Congeniality is voted on by the competitors only and is therefore a very special category. Your Miss Congeniality is," the emcee yells, "Courtney Gilbert!" The other two girls turn and clap at Courtney, and she waves. The emcees have fired through the categories—no pause, no ruminating. At horsemanship, though, they dwell a moment. "Horsemanship is one of the great and unique things a rodeo queen must do,"

51 During my time with the rodeo queens, I have been acutely aware of my shortcomings. I can't ride like they can, I understand only the basics of bull riding and cattle tying, and I know comparatively little about Idaho industry and agriculture. In this moment I am more sharply aware of these shortcomings than ever.

Though I take issue with MRI's narrow portrayal of the *ideal* woman and I am quick to question this flat interpretation of Idaho, beneath all my reason and logic and judgment, there rests a gut reaction to this culture. As Kacey circles the stage and sparkles in the light, I am smitten. I am five years old again, sitting in rodeo bleachers, watching the late sun catch in a queen's crown. And while all comparisons to the queens thus far have rendered me inferior, I cannot help but wonder about my compulsion to compare. I am less interested in my failings as this type of westerner and more concerned with my childlike infatuation, with my need to be sized up. Though I realize the MRI institution is only promoting a version of this place, a shadow of its former self, I know it's a version I'm also attached to.

an emcee says. Courtney shifts a little, Abby tips her hat down, and Kacey stares ahead. "And the winner is," the emcee allows a long delay, "Kacey Quibb." Kacey does not look surprised or overly excited. She steps forward, again, and waves. Kacey wins appearance. Kacey wins personality. Kacey wins speech. The emcees say her name with mock surprise, as if to say, "Kacey . . . again!"

The lights dim, and an emcee says, "Now we'll announce places." None of the girls moves or touches her hair or looks down. They stand, poised and posing, and stare into the light. Second runner-up will win 750 bucks, a bracelet, a Mary Kay body treatment package, and a host of other trinkets. The girls stare ahead, each praying her name isn't called. "Courtney Gilbert," the emcee shouts. Courtney steps forward and waves limply, and the emcee moves right along. The first runner-up will receive flowers, $1,000, a monogrammed equine set and grooming kit, plus a bag of horse feed. The emcee pauses for effect. "Your first place runner-up is," the emcee says quietly, "Abby Bowler." For a moment Abby does not move. She stares, dazed. Then she steps forward, and Kacey shakes and breathes hard. Abby takes her flowers and waves once more to the crowd, but as soon as she has returned to the lineup, Kacey steps into the light. "Your Miss Rodeo Idaho is," the emcee yells, "Kacey Quibb!" Kacey walks to the MRI president, takes her bouquet, and begins pacing the stage. Like her modeling routine, the walk is all circles. She takes tiny steps around the stage and beams and laughs. Then she walks to Amber, and Amber fixes the tiara on her hat, and Kacey rests a hand on her brim. "Idaho Cowgirl" plays again, and a pocket of people stands and applauds. Kacey stops, center stage, with the flowers resting across her chest, and tips her head back into the light.[51]

Press and Acting Duties

The queens are ushered backstage, where the First Lady of Idaho waits to take pictures with Kacey. Rather cruelly, Abby and Court-

52 Kacey spins on her boot heels, and the tiara sparkles from her hat brim, and a photographer fires away and tells her, "Great energy, gorgeous, tip the hat down. Show us that crown!" I stand in the corner of the room, skeptical of yet in a way deeply charmed by this woman on display. We are different creatures. But perhaps we are connected in this: on some level the queens and I both attempt to preserve this place. After all, it is my fascination with Idaho that compelled me to shadow these girls. We are both promoters offering a particular kind of story, our only difference being that I, unlike the queens, am not sure I fully understand what it means to be western. I know Idaho isn't all mountain peaks and farm fields. I am reluctant to accept the anecdotes about elementary principals (in church clothes!) rounding up stray bulls. I'm not sure the ideal woman is aged eighteen to twenty-five, single, and shimmering with rhinestones. I know that for every cowboy in Rigby, there's a computer engineer (or ten!) in Meridian. But I also appreciate those prototypical symbols (erroneously?) associated with my home, no matter how faulty or outdated: the smells of harvested mint in late summer, of horses lathered in sweat, of corn silking into ripeness. The electric buzz of cicadas at dusk; bullfrogs moaning through the night. I understand the allure of just-broke roans bucking in corrals, of spinning bulls and champion riders and queens jetting horseback around rodeo rings. And to write about this place is to offer my own version, and perhaps such writing is just another form of preservation.

ney must watch Kacey pose for headshots and shake hands. An *Idaho Statesman* reporter asks Kacey which prize she is most proud of. Standing backstage beneath dim neon lights, with smudged makeup and sagging curls, she doesn't hesitate. "Horsemanship," she says. "It really proves rodeo queens aren't just about the glamour." And with that, the reporter thanks her, and Kacey steps in front of the camera.

Courtney and Abby do not leave. They have one more meal with the judges, and then they will go home late tonight. Courtney is all smiles and relaxed. She is not weepy or angry or discouraged. "I just did this for practice for next year," she says. "Now I'll just read the judges' feedback and start prepping." And she does not say this in the forced way of most non-winners. She seems earnest. This was her game plan. Show up, then zero in on 2012. Abby, though, is heartbroken. She dabs a tissue beneath her eyelashes. Mascara runs, and she turns away. Courtney consoles her.

Kacey is amped on adrenaline. There is no grace in her victory. She laughs and fist pumps. She whips her hair and reapplies lipstick and asks the MRI president if her teeth are clean. When her mother comes backstage, Kacey runs across the room. They hug, and her mother runs her fingers over the crown. Then they high-five. Kacey does not console her fellow competitors. She does not tell them they did great or that they really brought the heat or that it was a really close one. She does not stroke the fallen queens' egos by reminding them that these things are subjective. *Could've easily been you.* None of that. Kacey stands in front of the photographer, a deep-blue curtain behind her, the tiara glowing from her hat, and smacks a wide, shining smile.[52]

The Wild Ones

A Reunion of Sorts

Grouped by age, the colts come first. Yearlings lean into one another, the herd mentality running deep: safety in numbers, move as a pack. Makeshift bridles run beneath their jaws. Hooked to the string, a tag with a number: 1529, 1917, 2460. White waves scar their hips; some haven't lost their winter coats; shag clumps on croups and bellies; sagebrush hang in tails—those remnants of wild. Taped to each pen, a bidding form.

The mustang is arguably the most familiar symbol of the West: beer commercials; rodeo posters; T-shirts puff-painted with stallions bolting across American flags; the most iconic U.S. sports car; the mascot of my high school; my neighbor's ankle tattoo; the subject of countless pop songs—*Couldn't drag us away*, sang the Stones, *May no man's touch ever tame*, warned Ray LaMontagne, *Throwing caution to the wind, I'll run free too*, promised Natasha Bedingfield.

The mustang (as an icon at least) seems inescapable. And though I grew up near the Owyhee Mountains, a stretch of high desert buttes home to Idaho's largest herd, until the Bureau of Land Management's (BLM) Wild Horse and Burro Adoption, I'd never been so close to the real deal.

The Western Idaho Fair has always been the raison d'être of a Treasure Valley summer. When I was a kid, the neighbors would band together and head out for elephant ears and beers and the Steve Miller Band. Now, though, Eagle's demographic has morphed. We are no longer the fair-going type. Even Eagle's own town festival, Eagle Fun Days, has changed. It used to be all about the Eagle Nut Feed—where locals would gather to eat those beef balls, sliced thin and fried, as delicious as calamari. Now the Nut Feed is seriously downplayed, slotted for a Thursday night, and each year a petition to shut it down circulates. Generally, the fair culture—homegrown radishes and blue-ribbon pies and slow carousels and Bud Lights—is a little too butter crusted and dusted out for Eagle folks anymore.

Lucky for me, I'm in town when the fair begins. For three weeks my afternoons have been long with river floats and bike rides and lunch dates. Each day I think of Tucson, and though I am thankful for the grass lawns of Boise and the cooler temps and cold river, I miss the way the Catalina Mountains blush at dusk, how the saguaro blossoms become silver palms of moonlight each night, and I think we are prone to romanticizing most every place, not just the ones that grew us. These idealizations become a way of refuting the details we'd rather skip over—the blistering heat, the cockroach burrowed in your pillow. They make our inevitable returns more palatable.

Every day I think of Ryan too. For so much of this trip, my cell phone has been pinned to my ear. Like a teenager ripped away for a family vacation, I just want to talk to my person. And a state fair is exactly the sort of thing Ryan would get behind—novelty food, cold beers, exceptional people watching. Our kind of a good time. Instead, I take one of my oldest friends, a blonde tattooist who lives in Boise's tree-lined North End. We buy tickets at the door and sneak beers in our purses. Inside the fairgrounds, the desert erupts with flashing lights and megaphoned carnies and the howling sirens of victorious ring tossers. Corndog stands and Tilt-a-Whirls. Packs of children sob into their cotton candy. Past the main entrance, a fountain splashes and tired mothers soak their feet, and in the bandstand a cover band sings Creedence Clearwater Revival numbers. No one stops at the stage, but at the end of "Proud Mary," the singer, a potbellied man wearing a tank top and a mullet, hits his knees and points to the passersby—a big finish. Behind the stage spreads a legion of mobile kitchens: pork pulls, elephant ears, Brooklyn deli, Chicago pizza, onion rings, curly fries, lemonade, slushies, Pronto Pups, Old West BBQ. The food court abuts a twenty-foot slide and a row of Wack-a-Moles. The rides go on forever: Ferris wheels, carousels, the Flying Scooter, three House of Mirrors, four rollercoasters, bumper cars, Big Circus Side Show, Dance Dance Revolution, Skydiver, Superman, SuperStar, the High Striker, the Yo-Yo, the Zipper. A petting zoo. Past the petting zoo, a barn stinking with livestock—pigs and sheep and cattle. In a corral ten-year-olds lead thousand-pound steers to the center of the ring. From the stands bidders holler and steers sell and children beam.

Behind the barn a dirt path bisects a field. Horses, tied to trailers, wait to be curried and saddled. A girl in brown braids runs barrels in a corral. George Strait wails on a pickup's radio and then, for a while, nothing. Just flat desert pasture—trampled grass and dandelion bulbs. An occasional breeze upsets cheatgrass and wild rye. The faint hollers of running children and the chugging of rollercoasters and the tinkle of carousel song are barely audible. The jangle and clang of the fair leaches out. In the far end of the field, invisible from the bumper cars and candied almond carts, stands a cluster of pens.

The horses have mellowed to the distant clatter, never whinnying or stirring at the strange song of fairgoers, their bells and sirens and whistles. Detached from the fair's roar, the whole scene stagnant.

Four corrals cluster together: a pen for colts, a pen for mares, one for geldings, one for burros. A few men pace around the animals, bending to check hooves, holding out hands to test dispositions. *That forelock's no good, that blaze means squirrely genes, socks might mean weak hooves.* A girl tugs her father's sleeve, begging, "She's only one hundred dollars." The animal is taller than the others, brushed down, combed shiny. Her father lures her away with the promise of sno-cones.

These few bidders and the flimsy pens are not what I'd imagined. I'd envisioned a ring full of strong horses galloping, the kind you'd see in a Chevy commercial; bleachers packed with buyers, dollars flying; auctioneers rattling. But this crowd, sparse to begin with, thinned quickly. Perhaps these halfhearted bidders are as surprised by the tired and mangy mustangs as I am. Google *wild mustang*, and images of muscled stallions flood the browser. Herds splash through mountain creeks; mares roll in wildflowers; colts whinny over crabgrassed hills; palomino harems shine. Here, though, the horses are bony, harried. Their hips jut at odd angles, their eyes crust over, their heads bend low, thin red bridles hook beneath their jaws.

A Theory on Why the Mustang Matters

The mustang is our mascot, our chosen representative. In it we see the West (and ourselves) as we like to imagine it: strong, rugged, wild. But these words are no truer for the wild horse than they are for this land of drive-thrus and strip malls. Even the name smacks of paradox: *mustang* literally meaning "the wild one." The irony is clear: mustangs, those emblems of western idealism (freedom, power, wildness), have been captured, harnessed, tamed, and now not a soul wants them.

Twenty years ago I rode through the Owyhee Mountains in the back of my father's pickup. It was spring, and the ground, so early in the morning, was packed with frost. Cattails shone white. I rode in the pickup's bed, my back against the window, and Bob Dylan whined from the truck's cab. The road was gutted from flash floods and melted snow; the truck shook down the washboard, and I braced against its tossing. We were just past the tree line—the foothills cresting beneath us, the snowline packed hard above. The canyon lay buried in dark, early shadows. On the crest of a high cliff, with new light breaking the horizon, one palomino, the color of cream, bent its head to the ground. Its mane hung in a blanched wave. The truck stopped. The mare eyed me. It tossed its head, sniffing the strange smells—gasoline and soap and dirty clothes. Bob Dylan sang on. It muscled a low, gentle whinny and walked down to the canyon from which we'd come.

I was born into horses, can remember looking eye level to my mare's chest, and I can't recall a time when I didn't know to mount on the left, to keep my reins taut, to speak gently when the ears pull back. Working his way through college, my father was a stable boy. When he moved west, he built a corral by his house, and beneath my bedroom window, horses sighed and bucked the whole night through.

In the summer, before school began, my father and I would trailer the horses and drive into the mountains. He'd park at a trailhead, and we'd ride all day and pitch a tent on a lakeshore. We'd wake to the sound of our mares hoofing through pine needles or whinnying at coyote song. My horse was my ticket to Idaho's remote corners, to solitude and adventure. So I've been a sucker for those Google pictures of mustangs cooling their bellies in river shallows.

Consequently, I came to the auction a little naively. When my friend and I realized there was a horse pen behind the food court, she'd wanted to leave. "They're going to sell mustangs?" she'd asked. "That just sounds wrong." I couldn't disagree with her; it seemed vulgar (tame any animal but the wild horse!), but I wanted to reclaim that brief moment in the Owyhees. I remembered the palomino on the hillside, how calmly it had eyed me, how that moment suspended and swelled.

Memory, we know, is an unruly master. I recall the adrenaline of jumping a horse over a creek bed, the rich smells of buffed leather and horse skin, the slow rhythm of tails swishing at flies, and nothing of the hard falls and muscle bruises or the headache of catching a runaway pony high in the Bitterroot Mountains or tossing hay on frozen nights, fingers cramped from the cold.

The Wild Ones   127

Those memories, faulty as they may be, are the cornerstones of my own story of this place, and to understand place, as we know, is to understand self. We look to the land (or its story), and we say that we are one and the same. If the land is rugged and sublime, we are its byproduct. If the cowboy is tough, we've got equal grit. If the mustang is untamable and powerful, so are we. And conversely, if the mustang has been caught and made un-wild, then so too, we have been taken out at the knees.

A Word on Sanctuaries

The auction is a chance to see the mustang as I'd always imagined it, to find a palomino as calm and patient as the one I'd encountered on that Owyhee hill. It is a chance to access a piece of my past. But the scene is all business. On the bidding grounds one woman runs the show. A tall, thick blonde with round cheeks and full lips—a looker by rodeo queen standards—she paces the pens. She points to a yearling and says how promising those hindquarters look. She asks the shoppers if they've ever had horses before, if they've ever broken a wild animal. She explains how important the BLM's work is. Wild horses have no predators, she explains, so they overpopulate quickly and overgraze land. *We are saving them from starvation, inbreeding, genetic deformities; we are preserving a piece of American pride, and we are offering it to you for the low price of $150!*

This is true-ish. Wild horses occupy the last scraps of the public range—federally owned expanses in almost all of the eleven western states, and their presence is really divisive. Some consider the mustang a national treasure worthy of federal protection, while cattle ranchers see the horse as a thief of valuable grassland.

In an attempt to give the ranchers land and appease mustang advocates, the BLM rounds up the ponies and stores them in holding facilities, which they call, affectionately, "sanctuaries"—a weird word, not just because it conjures holiness but also because it can mean "an immunity to arrest," or, put another way, a refusal to be tamed, which is, of course, the opposite of what's happening here. Wild horse advocates are quick to question the sanctuaries. Deanne Stillman, in her book *Mustang: The Saga of the Wild Horse in the American West*, points out that in nature the horses do indeed have predators, mountain lions and wolves. What the BLM ought to say, rather, is that the horses in the sanctuaries have no predators and the sanctuaries are overcrowded.

Some of these horses had been to auction three or four times. After their fourth trip, they are held until they meet the criteria for euthanasia. The criteria include lameness, severe tooth loss or wear, inability to keep up with peers, or exhibiting dangerous characteristics. Not surprisingly, protestors identify these criteria as vague and subjective, but after the Bush administration approved a carte blanche killing policy on the animals, the federally run horse facilities seem to be a compromise—one that is hated by the cattle lobby (couldn't they just gun the horses down themselves?) and tolerated by wild horse advocates begrudgingly. In the sanctuaries the cattlemen see ghastly government intrusion, and the horse activists see a slaughterhouse.

The Part Where We Tear Apart the Theory That Mustang Equals West

The month of the BLM adoption, an acquaintance of my father's was found dead in his trailer. Feet up in his recliner, he'd been dead for three years. He lived alone in the hills outside the Treasure Valley and kept a small ranch with a few horses he'd bred and trained. He was a man who took to the hills and kept the company of horse and cattle and bucked society's comforts. He was a man who had failed (perhaps gloriously) to evolve. In those three years his herd multiplied—roans and duns unaccustomed to the smell of a human, the deep rub of a currycomb, the heft of a saddle. Here I see a new kind of wild, a return.

Another state, another headline. Two days after Christmas in 1998, outside Reno, Nevada, a hiker discovered thirty-four dead wild horses. All the horses had been shot; a few had been mutilated with fire extinguishers, eyes blasted from sockets, muzzles split open. Not all had died instantly. Some had dug holes into the frozen ground trying to pull themselves up. The event became known as the Wild Horse Massacre, and it brought new attention to the dilemma of the mustang. It definitely wasn't the first killing of its kind; pissed-off cattlemen had been shooting them for years, and cowboys had been selling wild horses to slaughterhouses for a hot dime since the 1800s.

Despite the familiarity of the crime, Nevada's prosecution posed a revolutionary argument, and here I am most interested. The district attorney asked, "How much is a wild horse worth?" The attorney went on to collect estimated dollar values of each horse. If the murdered horses were worth over $5,000, the boys on trial could be charged with a felony (the thirty-four horses were appraised, with little explanation, at $6,656). Like a team of mustangers rounding up a herd for dog food, the DA had reduced the mustang to a per-pound ticket price.

Everything has its price. Land, water, animals, they are all goods bartered and fought for. And the West has always been looted. We've commodified every bit of this "abundant," "free" land, and we realize nothing is less free than a commodity. Now cattlemen fight the mustang for prairie access, a new frontier war.

To talk about the mustang in dollar amounts is oxymoronic given the animal's associations with freedom and wildness. In the American West maybe no other animal (resource?) has been so exploited.

A Brief History of Exploitation

After Cortez returned the horse from Europe in the 1500s (the Ice Age had erased it from North America), the mustang boomed.

Once Europeans arrived, they collected them en masse, and the South fostered a deep relationship with horses; one of its greatest assets in the Civil War was its elevated horsemanship. The Union realized that if it were to contend, it had to match the South pony for pony, so it conducted the first official roundup. By the end of the war, one and a half million horses had died, and the mustang population took the biggest hit.

After the war, as cattle ranching boomed, wild horses were trained as cow ponies. Buffalo Bill began his Wild West Shows. Mustangs traveled the world and represented a way of life that was already disappearing. Then the horse birthed that ultimate western enterprise, Hollywood. Millionaire Leland Stanford famously bet that at some point during a thoroughbred's gallop, all four of its legs would lift off the ground. He enlisted the eccentric Eadweard Muybridge to document a horse's gallop. Muybridge created motion picture, and the first clip showed a horse's legs tucked in midair, the horse captured in flight. Soon enough, westerns (using mustangs that had actually herded cattle or fought in the Plains Wars) dominated the film industry. For centuries the mustang had experienced an uninterrupted succession of demand.

A Note on Death and Evolution

To call the wild horse "untamable" or "free" or even "wild" is sort of absurd given its exhaustive history of commodification. So in the mustang I don't see wildness but a metaphor for death.

When something (a person, a place, a narrative) evolves, it keeps traces of its former self, at least for a while. There's a comfort in this, as though the old story's death isn't totally final, or at least not immediately. It isn't vanishing—at least not right away; it's just morphing. But maybe in the wild horse we see an exception. Whites collected mustangs en masse, nearly obliterating wild herds, and instantly transformed them into war ponies, cow cutters, Hollywood stars. So in the mustang's taming there is no opportunity for evolution. There is just a dead end, a final stop. An animal can either be wild or it can be broken, and that is that.

By the mid-twentieth century the horse had become obsolete. The railroad and automobiles connected East and West; combines harvested farms; wars were fought with tanks and jets; the western film's popularity declined. Finally, the horse could return to the plains free.

For three years the horses ran the hills behind the dead man's trailer. They grazed and foaled and bolted from backfiring pickups and whistling hikers.

Regardless of the mustang's mythic appeal, once the horse failed to serve a monetary purpose, it became threatened. Some ranchers formed a movement (still popular in these parts today) known as the Sagebrush Rebellion. The government, at the behest of the rebels, poisoned the West through a program called Predator Control. Wild horses were shot and laced with strychnine, bait for any animal that might disturb cattle. For twenty years the government dappled the hillside with shotgun shells and poisoned water wells. "A wild horse consumes forage needed by domestic livestock, brings in no return, and serves no useful purpose," said a grazing service spokesman in 1939. Some fifty years later Congressman David Brower added, "Public land forage policies should be designed to attain maximum economic efficiency." Stillman sums it up: "Animals that depended on public land for sustenance but did not yield income, such as wild horses and burros, did not have a chance of survival."

The palomino muscled a low whinny and walked down to the canyon from which we'd come.

How the Mustang Reps the West, Example 2

The wild horse, experiencing no market demand, is rounded up and auctioned off. And isn't it weird that now that the horse serves no financial purpose, we force commodification on it by selling it to the highest bidder? We sell mustangs hoping someone still considers them worth something, anything.

I ask the BLM employee if people protest the auctions. "Oh sure," she says, laughing. "Anytime the government intervenes, you're going to tick somebody off." She says nothing of the BLM's controversial practices. She does not mention the helicopter roundups, which can be watched on the internet and are terrifying. The choppers nearly mow the poor creatures down. She does not discuss the lamed foals or neglected herds or the sanctuaries' conditions. Stillman reports that on one occasion the workers failed to feed the horses and clean out their pens. A blizzard froze the animals in their own muck; hundreds of horses died. Instead, the BLM employee offers a hand to a yearling, and the young horse quivers its lips to her palm.

The BLM agent's response, though evasive, hits an important point. This is the land of the outlaw, the Sagebrush Rebel, a world of self-regulation and big government hatred. *We run our own show.* The irony being, of course, that in the first decades of white settlement, the West was entirely subsidized by the American government, more socialist than self-regulated. *Anytime the government intervenes, you're going to tick somebody off.* The BLM agent does not question this resistance; it is, so often, a fact of Idaho living.

But most ranchers welcome any government meddling that helps them access grazing land, even if it means the demise of the wild horse. In this I see another fundamental dilemma in the old model. The story paints westerners as a self-governed, minimally regulated people (real badasses, actually); it asserts that land and animals and other resources are only dirtied by federal protection. Stereotypical westerners refuse regulation, but then the things that have for so long defined this place—buckskins grazing through belly-high grass—disappear. By being "western" we obliterate the West that lured us here.

In Idaho's wilderness I have seen hawks, falcons, eagles, deer, moose, foxes, coyotes, cougars, elk, bobcats, black bears, rattlesnakes coiled on melon gravel, but only once the palomino at daybreak.

Insiders, Outsiders, and Why We Don't Like Your Kind

In those years when my father and I took to the hills and spotted antelope and peregrines and once the wild palomino, I rode my mare with the frequency and nonchalance of a child on her bike. This was when homes in Eagle sat on ten acres or more and most every kid had a pony. After school we'd dump our backpacks and head to the corral. By the mid-nineties the farm fields that surrounded our own mini-farms were paved for themed subdivisions—those mock-Italian villas or Malibu-esque ranch houses, huge homes on lots large enough for a trampoline or Slip 'N Slide but nothing more, no corral or barn or pasture. I rode my horse down the just-dried sidewalks, and the neighbors stared from their picture windows.

Insiders versus outsiders, newcomers against old-timers, it's the first story of this place. The cattle lobby has claimed wild horses are "feral newcomers to this country (varmints), and therefore protecting them would be the same as protecting alley cats or invasive weeds." The horse, the cattle lobby argued, has no claim to this land.

The Rebels deny the genetic findings that link horses to their pre–Ice Age ancestors, and thus the wild horse has come to represent our collective insistence on nativism. A silly fight, really, given that perhaps nothing better characterizes the West than constant influx. To argue that the wild horse is not native and therefore does not deserve access to the land ignores the fact that few westerners are native. This is a place of constant population swells, of just-arrived newcomers.

It also ignores, more problematically, our ugly history. In any conversation about nativism, there's no gliding by the indigenous people who are the sole heirs to that title. White people's presence here is defined by our stealing, displacement, violence, and erasure. Children torn from parents. Blankets laced with smallpox. Massacres and massacres and massacres.

When we talk about nativism, we should be talking about shame.

Give Me Land, Lots of Land; Let Me Wander over
Yonder, 'cause I Can't Look at Hobbles and
I Can't Stand Fences; So Send Me Off Forever
but I Ask You Please, Don't Fence Me In
(Or: The Trouble with Taming)

My father took a horse from the dead man's hills. Someone had rounded them up and was selling them off, and my father liked a two-year-old chestnut with a watcheye and white socks. He filled his palm with grain, looped a lead line around its neck, wrestled on a bridle, and drove it home to his corral.

When I was nine, my mare foaled. Before dawn my mother shook me awake, and I ran to the barn to find my father lying in the straw with the just-born horse, slick and bluish and eyes tight shut. My father's body curved around it so it would know his smell and touch, so it would be born tamed.

Not with the chestnut. The chestnut had been wild for too long. After my father took it from the dead man's pasture, he worked it each night, starting with lead line and blanket and curries. He'd rub his hands down the animal's back, speaking in low tones, soothing him as he held the hoof, as he rubbed the underbelly. Soon it would come in to the sound of grain shaking in a bucket. Soon my father would add harness and bridle, saddle and rein.

Like the cowboy, the mustang is a common feature of our collective identity. After all, Americans everywhere buy Ford sports cars, drink Budweiser, listen to pop music. Marketers understand our partiality to our de facto mascot. In popular iconography the mustang is paired with western sunsets *or* American flags. The mustang charms all of America. And doesn't all of this (our need for a shared story, for a representation that flatters, for a story that explains ourselves) extend beyond the West and westerners? Isn't all of this part of being a society, part of being human?

The mustang symbolizes the West, as most everyone would agree, but not in the super majestic ways we like to imagine (all that wildness, strength, freedom, etc.). Instead, in the mustang I see a West unflattered. I see the human need to commodify—everything, it seems, animals, land, nature itself. Or I see our hypocritical insistence on limited government. Or our (hypocritical again) fixation with nativism. So we dream about mustangs, and we insist that the animals embody what it means to be American—which is another way of saying they reflect who we are—and we fail to acknowledge the really ugly ways in which this is true.

And right now the ugliest truth I see in the mustang is its brokenness, for here we are forced to acknowledge our own taming. Most westerners, something like 80 percent, live in the suburbs. This is the ultimate picture of reining in—taking a prairie and fencing it into a million quarter-acre pens with tended lawns and poisoned weeds and clipped hydrangeas and smooth sidewalks. And as a result of this tidy, square-lawned living, few westerners know how to interact with any kind of wildness—animals, land, anything. I don't know how to get food that isn't served in a restaurant or grocery store or how to go rogue in the woods without my Sterno and tent, for example. And here, perhaps, is where our affection for the mustang is most potent and most beguiling. If we quit this romance and opt for reality, we'll see that the mustang is tamed, and then we'll see that we're tamed, and then we'll be really bummed out because there is nothing more dangerous (disappointing? heartbreaking?) to the western identity than being broken.

Nobody wants these mustangs. The auction half over, all the bidding forms are blank. There is no cloud cover, no wind, and the temperature has spiked. The horses flick their tails at flies, look to the ground for water but find dirt. No dogwoods or cottonwoods or maples shade the meadow. Everyone sweats in their boots.

People don't hang around the auction for long. Some parents heard there were baby horses in a pen and brought their children to see—an extension of the petting zoo, they assumed. Those that are semi-interested in buying an animal scan the pens and return to the food court, anxious for shade trees and lemonade. I lean against a corral, a sorrel brushing her tail against my calf, and imagine speeding a pickup through the fair, past all those strobe-lit rides and pork pull stands. I imagine mothers pushing strollers out of my way. I'd pull a trailer to the meadow and wave off the buxom BLM beauty. I'd spring these horses yet. I'd drive them deep into the desert, all the way to the Snake River, and let them drink and splash in a slow current.

But How about a Little Love for the Cowboy?

While I obviously take issue with the BLM's adoptions, I don't intend to belittle the cattlemen's plight. Their struggle is most evident in Nevada, where the bulk of wild horses remain and where much cattling is still done. Ranchers are private businesspeople, and their operations are expensive and often reap zero dividends. The last thing they need is a herd of horses stealing their feed.

But some folks claim the actual effect of the wild horse on the cattle industry isn't so clear-cut. The *Territorial Enterprise*, in Virginia City, Nevada, reports, "In view of the practically unlimited grazing land available in Western Nevada and the absurdly small number of horses, such claims are purely fictional." Mustang advocates argue that the horse actually increases forage by spreading seeds through their manure, and as Patricia Nelson Limerick points out in her book *The Legacy of Conquest: The Unbroken Past of the American West*: "Wild animals roam, rotating their grazing pressure from place to place; domestic animals, according to the wills of their herders, often stay too long in one place, depleting the plants and their capacity to regenerate. Wild animals, if their range becomes drastically overstocked, will die off until the numbers and the resources rebalance; domestic animals can have populations maintained too long at artificially high levels." Mustangs are the ultimate self-regulators, then, able to control their consumption and population in relation to the health of the land.

Even if the wild horse really is bringing these cowboys down, their economic effect deserves examination. According to the *San Jose Mercury News*, the wild horse's impact on national beef demand cannot be too drastic. These days only 3 percent of beef production occurs in the West. *Brings in no return, and serves no useful purpose*, said Congress of the mustang. If we accept the argument that only those animals that reap fiscal rewards may lay claim to the land, then we must question the worth of cattle. If the mustang can be obliterated on the grounds of lacking any economic purpose, then so too, the western cattle industry, meeting a sliver of the market's demand, is nearly equally dispensable on the national level.

Because these ranches satisfy so little of the market's needs, they rely heavily on federal subsidies—a dependence that undercuts any notions of government separation cowboys might like to harbor. If we satisfy the myth through true self-governing, then both mustang and cowboy, cherished symbols of this place, die off. Without regulation the cowboy will take out the mustang, and the hardships of the free market will wipe out the cowboy.

Mustangs, Cowboys, and Why We're Actually All in This Together

When I was six, my father brought home a Jersey the color of weak coffee (this was the same cow I sobbed over at the dinner table). Despite my mother's warnings, I named the calf. I brought it salt licks and fed it grain from my palm. I'd saddle Misty, and Little Dot would walk beside us. The pasture became prairie, Little Dot a longhorn, Misty a mustang–turned–cow horse. How inseparable the model of the cowboy and the mustang remain, how enmeshed their roots.

The story of the mustang and the rancher is one of death: the mustang brought to near extinction, the western cattle industry nearly obsolete. They are proof that this story is old and tired and best be laid to rest. They are reminders that if we cling to a dead thing, we can't evolve. But to abandon the old story is terrifying. After all, it's our stories that allow us to understand ourselves. If the mustang is tamed, if the rancher is obsolete, then we are bereft, destabilized, unable to insinuate ourselves into the company of a shared mythology—or even worse, we must face the ways in which we no longer satisfy the story; we're left to stare down our own taming. Without the comforts of a known story, we are left searching for a new narrative, one without the stoic independence of the cowboy or the beauty of palominos grazing on canyon bluffs. But the new story would be a true one, and maybe that should be enough.

Another Note on Death

As President Nixon fought for the Free-Roaming Wild Horse and Burro Act of 1971, he said, by way of Thoreau, "We need the tonic of wildness." Nixon went on, "In the past seventy years, civilization and economics have brought the horse to 99% extinction . . . They merit protection as a matter of ecological right—as anyone knows who has stood awed at the indomitable spirit and sheer energy of a mustang running free." Three years after Nixon endorsed the wild horse (and before Reagan overturned the act), stockmen in Howe, Idaho, out on the desert-plained, Wyoming side of the state, chased down a herd. They drove the horses into a narrow canyon, rushed them down shale walls at breakneck speeds. The animals fled, only to run out of valley. The horses flew up on an iced-over cliff. Many jumped; others crashed into rocks. Some lamed over fallen tree trunks or gopher holes. Others panicked, breaking legs as they clamored for safety. By the end only six horses survived, and the ranchers strung hog rings into their nostrils and led them away. Within days they were shipped to Nebraska for slaughter, a slight profit turned.

After working a horse, my father would return it to pasture. *Never leave them with the bridle,* he'd cautioned me. Always remove lead lines and reins. Set them to pasture tackless, naked. They could trip on rope; their bridles could catch on tree branches.

After my father lunged the new chestnut, it would bolt from the corral slick with sweat. One night, though, my father found it tethered to a fence post. He'd removed its tack, but it was caught nonetheless. Its tail had tangled in barbed wire, and it had tried to free itself with its back leg. Bone shined through. My father got his gun.

The silent auction lasts two hours. At the end only two animals were claimed: a short, heavy-coated burro and a roan mare. The

BLM agent pulls the bidding forms from the pens. The buyers lean against trailers, filling out paperwork. A woman approaches the new owners, peddling handmade bridles, twenty dollars apiece, any color you want. The man with the roan chooses forest green and wrestles it up the animal's face, taking extra care with the ears. He smooths the thatch of hair and clips a lead line to the bridle.

On my way back to the fair, I stop by the yearling's pen. All chestnuts, the afternoon sun shines on their backs. The horses, accustomed to the poking and prodding of BLM employees or halfhearted bidders, don't stir when I approach. I hold out a hand, and one brave colt buries its muzzle deep in my palm. I stroke the muscled croup and ribbed belly. I let it rub its forelock against my arm, scratching some deep, unreachable itch.

A Wild Horse Hunt

My last week in Idaho is precisely planned: a few family dinners, one more slice of pizza at Flying Pie, a movie at the Flicks. I'll take my niece to the cupcakery, and we will eat cake pops by the river. All that, and I want to go on a ride with my dad. At dawn he peels away my blanket, and I rise and follow him to the barn.

The BLM claims only one herd remains in Idaho, 150 horses in the Owyhee Mountains. After little state-mandated regulation and decades of two-steps-forward-one-step-back legislation, ranchers have nearly wiped the mustang from Idaho's prairie. But the fate of the horse in Idaho, locals know, isn't quite so grim. Shadow Butte—thirty minutes from Eagle in the high desert stretch near Oregon, just past Emmett's apple orchards—is home to a clutter of horses. Stop by the Cloverleaf on Emmett's main drag, and anybody will tell you they know a rancher in those hills who sees them bastards come down every day. My father and I bank on that regularity.

Like most of these hills, Shadow Butte is gray in winter, green in spring, gold in summer. A few ranch homes line the road up the mountain. Sheepdogs thump tails at our passing. Trail horses pace their pens. The road fades from pavement to washboard, and we drive farther up, past trail turnoffs and side roads, beyond the grazing cattle, until the hillside looks wild again.

We saddle our mares and take to the first hill. Our horses cut through sagebrush and creek beds, and grass turns to lava rock. We ride on. At the steepest summit my saddle loses its cinching. I feel it loosen, and when I shift to stay level, the grade pulls me over. I roll down the bluff, knocking hips and shoulders on lava rock. I stand, and the hills spin. My mare flicks her tail at horseflies, waiting patiently, and I pull cheatgrass from my hair and remount.

Heat settles in. The sun blazes; sweat pools; my wrists and legs bleed. A plum lump rises on my elbow. We've ridden high up the butte and seen nothing. A few deer had scattered from a wash, and that was all. No grazing harems, no loping stallions. Sore and aching, I steer my mare back. "I think we've struck out," I yell to my father. He turns his bay, and we reverse out of the bluffs.

I am nauseated from hitting the rocks, embarrassed at taking such a stupid fall. I have fallen from horses before, broken bones, bruised ribs, but I have been bucked or tossed mid-jump. This time my horse was standing still, waiting kindly as I tried to regain my balance. And I just fell. My father, after he consoled me, admitted it was the slowest, sorriest fall he'd ever seen, truly pathetic. I feel distant from my Idaho roots, as though it was my first time in the saddle, as if I'd never seen a horse before, as if the palomino on the bluff was of no consequence, as if this story had had no bearing on whom I've become. If my home is a place of wild horses and tough cowgirls, then I should be able to ride this old mare up a hill. But I can't. I've lost my ruggedness, can't even stay in the saddle—proof of my own taming, I suppose.

Clouds cover the butte, a few more deer wander away from us, and just before the trailer comes into sight, I slow my horse. My father pulls his reins. We wait. From the slope of some unseen hill comes a deep pounding, horses loping, hoofbeats on the prairie.

I remember slouching in the pickup bed and riding up that Owyhee hill. I remember how dawn flamed the hillside, how the frost shone, how the palomino waited, and then, at its choosing, how it left me.

All my life I have carried the palomino grazing at the top of the Owyhee canyon with me. I remember the hard jostle of the gravel road, the frost-spackled truck bed, Bob Dylan wailing, "It Ain't Me, Babe"—yet I am certain this never happened. On Sunday mornings, more often than not, I sat in church with my mother. And if I had set out into the hills with my father on an early spring morning, we would have been in the Eagle foothills, just five minutes from our home, and we would have been on horseback. What's more, I can't imagine what would have possessed me, at six years old, to brave the low temps of an April morning in the back of my father's pickup for the hour-long drive it takes to break deep into the Owyhees. It couldn't have happened. Yet somehow I have told myself a story about finding a palomino in the green hills of Idaho and smelling the sage together.

Remembering and fabricating are essentially interchangeable. But what I'm most interested in isn't just that my memory failed but that I chose to tell myself a particular story, one mired in the old version of this place. And what's even weirder is that even though I know the old model is busted, that the palomino was an apparition, I scaled Shadow Butte hopeful for mustangs, attempting to regain something I felt I'd lost.

We come to the myth hoping to understand who we are, so admitting that the palomino was a dream is like holding a glassless mirror to my face and expecting a reflection. If the story is gone, we are adrift, rootless, unsure of who we are and how to proceed. If the mustang is tamed, then we're forced to look inward and face our own taming (the pen-like quarter-acre lots of Eagle, my inability to stay in the saddle). So I rode out of those hills and cleaned my scrapes, nursed my bruises, and told myself, maybe halfheartedly, it had been worth it. We had heard something: the unprovable rhythm of something unseen, something unknowable. But maybe those hoofbeats were just another story we'd told ourselves, something transpired out of our deep hopefulness, out of our abiding need for those animals to be there, for these stories to be true.

Ladies' Night at the Shooting Range

The man at the counter is everything I expect: a mustache, an American flag T-shirt, revealingly snug jeans. A Glock .45 strapped to his waist, it is massive, a thing of action films. The weapons make me uneasy. They surround me. It feels like they could go off with zero prompting, phantom trigger fingers rocketing bullets from their chambers.

"What brings you shooting?" he asks.

The walls are lined with shotguns and rifles; cabinets loaded with steely revolvers; mounted in a corner, a flintlock the color of sawdust. I am wearing a dress, pink ballet flats, eye shadow. In my purse, a postmodern novel. I leave for Tucson tomorrow morning, and tonight I'll have a final dinner with my family; this afternoon I'll meet friends for one last game of bocce ball. But here, before all that, I have carved a few hours for myself.

"Any particular reason?" he asks again.

"Just curious." I stare into the glass case, all those pistols shining.

On my eighth birthday my father brought my gift in from the garage. Camouflage flecked the box. A girl cast a fishing line, and a river rolled away from her. A wide-mouthed trout leaped from the rapids. LIL' ANGLERS FISHING KIT stamped on the box.

When I was three, my family camped on the shores of Warm Lake. We ate what we caught, and I stood behind my brother as he cast off. When he flung the line over his shoulder, the hook sunk into my scalp.[1] My father snatched me up and carried me off to the campfire. He pinned me between his knees, his boots digging into my ribs, keeping me still. I heard his Leatherman snap open. He said the hook sunk to the skull. After he sliced it out, he bent down and flattened his palm. The metal shone with blood, and a few of my hairs stayed stuck.

I balled up the wrapping paper and put the box down.

"Open it," he said.

I slid apart the cardboard. No fishing pole—relief. Mock-wood plastic and a cold metal barrel, its body the color of chestnuts, filigree etched into the bolt. I felt the gun's balance in my palms. Tied to the barrel hung a pack of BBs, shining and silver like tiny comets. I swung it to my shoulder and closed one eye, just as I'd seen my father do. The trigger curved against my finger.

I hadn't asked for the air rifle, but this was the year I discovered *The Good, the Bad, and the Ugly*. My brother and I watched Clint Eastwood's Blondie squint and smoke his cigar, his hand never far from his six-shooter. We took to our pasture, paced off, and pointed our water guns.

My mother was less excited about the gift. "Don't point it in the house," she cautioned. "Tom, tell her not to point it."

"Only point when you mean to shoot, and always keep the safety on."

"And never inside the house," my mother added.

But guns were all over our home. Mounted in the basement, a rifle my grandfather and father had built together. In the hallway a Revolutionary War flintlock my mother had inherited. Locked away in their bedroom closet, a cabinet of pistols and shotguns, my father's collection. Guns as relics, as heirlooms; guns for hunting or protection. I swung my air rifle over my shoulder and walked to the porch, my father leading the way.

Every sensible gun owner knows when buying an air rifle, there is only one option. Since 1886 Daisy has been the premier BB gun manufacturer. Clarence Hamilton, a low-level worker at a windmill company, created a gun that would fire a lead ball using compressed air. The executive of the windmill replied with an emphatic, "Boy, that's a daisy!" He closed down windmill production and switched to air gun manufacturing. Soon enough, Daisies were flying down assembly lines, and fathers brought the mini-rifles home to their kids. A generation of gunslingers was born.

My father lined up three empty Coke cans on our split-rail fence. He poured the BBs into the mouth of the gun and pumped the lever fast. He raised it to his shoulder and hunched. I envisioned him high in the mountains, hunting elk or bear. I'd seen him trailer the horses and hop in his pickup, his rifle leaning in the seat beside him. He'd be gone for weeks, tracking game in the high corners of Idaho's Rocky Mountains. I pictured him riding a narrow ridge, his mare stiffening at a strange scent, and he would tuck the rifle to his shoulder.

My father pulled the trigger. A quick ping, and the soda can flew from the fence. "Now you." He handed me the gun, and I pumped hard, the lever more resistant each time.

"Keep that eye shut. When you're ready, take a nice big breath and exhale slowly. Then ease back the trigger."

I drew one breath and held it. I closed both eyes. My parents' yard of birches and cottonwoods disappeared. I saw Clint Eastwood saddled on his bay. A man in black crested the ridge. Blondie pulled his gun, and in a flash the trigger tugged, the bullet flew, the bad man fell.

I exhaled and pulled back my finger. The can spun and collapsed, that bright round pop.

I played with my gun in the same compulsive way most kids played video games or talked on the phone. Every night I rode my mare through Eagle's farm fields, my gun strapped to my side, and I suc-

cumbed to the vivid imaginings of childhood. A pioneer, an outlaw, a sheriff with a heart of gold and steady trigger finger. In each
iteration I was a woman whose pluck was made manifest by the
rifle strung to her saddle.

I packed empty soda cans and lined them on fences or hay bales.
When I ran out of cans, I tacked target sheets to tree trunks. I'd
save the sheets, a cluster of holes at the bull's eye, and show them
to my father.

"Pretty sharp shooter," he'd say, squeezing my arm.

Growing up in Idaho, I was always aware of the shoot-'em-up heroes
that haunt this place. Their names were never far from my reach,
and while other kids obsessed over basketball heroes or action film
stars, I studied the West's quick drawing, sharp shooting men and
women—outlaws and showmen, cowboys and criminals, all typ-
ified by the holster on their hip. Wild Bill Hickok. Calamity Jane.
Billy the Kid. Kid Curry. Wyatt Earp. Doc Holliday. Buckskin Les-
lie. Annie Oakley blasting apples from men's heads.

Like the mustang, the gun is a familiar symbol of this place. The
idea of the Wild West is dominated by the six-shooter just sprung
from an outlaw's holster, and in Idaho this story has been particularly true. Wyatt Earp, of Tombstone fame, settled in northern
Idaho with hopes of striking it rich in the Coeur d'Alene gold rush.
Three years after his showdown in the Arizona desert, Earp became
a businessman, selling tents to miners and running dance halls. A
hero in Tombstone, Earp's luck shifted in Idaho. The line between
hero and outlaw blurred. Local miner A. J. Pritchard accused Earp
of jumping his gold claim. Earp contested the accusation, but when
Pritchard revealed that two men, armed with Earp's revolvers, had
forcibly taken possession of the land, Earp's defense was blown.

I imagined the famed sheriff riding through the Bitterroots in
early autumn, the mountain peaks just silver with snow. In the river

shallows, pans glittered with gold. Earp dismounted. Pritchard, knee-deep in the quick current, drew his gun, but Earp drew faster. The flash of a pearl-handled six-shooter. The smoke of a spent cartridge. The glint of gold flecks in Earp's palm.

Two years later outlaw Butch Cassidy stirred dust at the other end of the state. In 1886 Montpelier, Idaho (just a few hours south of Howe, where those mustangs were run down), burst with hayfields. Settlers were crowding the state, fencing in Appaloosas and cattle, and alfalfa was in high demand. A booming farm town meant a booming bank, and Cassidy, the Sundance Kid, and the Wild Bunch set up camp on the other side of the Wyoming border and made plans.

In the peak of afternoon heat, the men rode into Idaho and hitched their horses outside the bank. One of the gang stood outside the door, pointing his gun into the street, warning the locals against trying anything brave. Cassidy drew his revolver and headed straight for the banker. The Sundance Kid waved his six-shooter toward the wall. The customers lined up. He kept his barrel level on the crowd. Cassidy packed saddlebags with silver coins and gold nuggets. He backed out of the bank, his gun raised and steady.

The men galloped their horses all the way back to Wyoming, their pistols snug at their hips.

I imagined these gunslingers as I rode Misty through hayfields and horse pastures. Each time I raised my gun, it was as though I were accessing something larger than myself, a history (tradition? inheritance?) entrenched in this place. The field just beyond our property was littered with abandoned cars. A 1950s Chevy sunk in the grass. Rust pocked a dust-blue paint job; its tires sagged beneath rims. It was neglected, abandoned. Nobody would notice. I pulled Misty's reins and brought my Daisy to my cheek. I'd never shot anything but scrap metal and targets. This was a violation, a broken law. I drew a long breath and pointed at the windshield. I lined up the sights. I squeezed the trigger. The windshield splintered. Glass tinkled like ice. That burst of velocity from my gun's barrel, the sound of a target hit, a transgression made. Butch Cassidy sped his horse through the Idaho desert, silver jingling in his pockets, his six-shooter still hot.

The same year my father gifted me the gun, my sister brought home a boy. He was captain of the football team, round faced, blue-eyed, all-American in that stereotypical way. He was a boy eager to win over a girl's family. When he heard I spent my evenings shooting hay bales, he offered to take me to the desert. "Let you shoot a real gun," he said.

Alex pulled into our driveway in the early morning, his truck packed with Eagle High football players. My father had talked up my aim, told him I was a sure shot. I was nervous.

I was just old enough to blush when one of the boys helped me into the pickup's bed. I sat next to a redheaded linebacker clutching a double-barreled shotgun. The wood was real, polished and bracketed with brass slabs. The metal thicker than my Daisy's, the trigger wider, the body longer, it was enormous.

Alex stopped the truck in a flat stretch of Idaho foothills, all dust and sage. The redhead jogged across the plain, clay discs in hand. Alex loaded the gun, snapped the barrel into place, and raised it to his shoulder. "Pull," he yelled. The disc shot up and soared—a level trajectory. Alex tugged, and the clay shattered. Fireworks in a pale sky. Again and again, the shotgun cracked, and the discs splintered.

"You try," he said.

The gun was heavier than I could handle. I shimmied it to my shoulder. Once it was tucked deep in my arm, I drew a long breath, pinched my eye shut. "Pull," I said. Just above the horizon, the black dot flew above me. I fired. The gun kicked. No crack of shot on clay. My face burned, and my arm cramped, and I felt the knot forming just above my armpit. I lowered the gun and lifted my sleeve—a half-moon already darkening. The pigeon thudded in the dust.

My arm throbbing, I heard my father telling Alex I had dead aim. All those football players stared at me, watching my arm swell and darken. "You all right, kid?" the redhead asked. I willed myself from tears.

The next night I rode Misty through the pasture and kept my BB gun level in my lap. It felt light, a cheap toy. I had shot Alex's gun a few more times, each time the rifle's butt kicking deeper into my bruise. By the end of the day I could nail a paper target, but I never hit a pigeon. Never that full shattering like the boys delivered. Back home, the Daisy in my lap, Blondie and Wyatt and Butch seemed like a joke, my gun a fake.

Just as my BB gun became lame and kid-like, it also seemed terrifying. My friend's father stretched out his arm.

"Feel this," he said, turning his palm up. He guided my finger over the plane of his arm. Just above his wrist, a hard lump shifted. "I've had that BB for thirty years."

My cheap, weak little gun had sufficiently freaked me out. After school I'd change into playclothes and leave it tucked behind my bedroom door.

Each fall my father grew restless. The mountains outside his office window, lit with autumn reds, pulled him from the Treasure Valley. Home from work, he'd blast the Traveling Wilburys and rummage in the garage, stuffing Duofolds and canteens into an army bag.

"Going hunting?" I asked.

"Better believe it. Want to come?"

The idea of killing an animal horrified me. I saw the limp-necked deer my father brought home, felt their hides still gritty with dirt. I saw the pictures of him kneeling over collapsed elk, the rack braced in his grip. We played board games and watched movies on the bearskin he brought down from the mountains. I was careful to never sit near its hollowed head. My parents slept beneath a mounted elk, its rack too large to fit in any room but theirs. When I was flu-ridden and dozing in their bed, I avoided its glassy stare.

I had never aimed for an animal, wouldn't risk a groundhog or magpie, but my father had never taken any of his children hunting, and I wanted to ride my horse up those loose-rocked cliffs and watch the elk, shaggy with new fur, wade through mountain streams.

We drove to the Frank Church Wilderness Area, south of the Bitterroots, north of the Sawtooths. We loaded our horses and a pack mule weighed down with cans of beans and a spare rifle. We spent the first day riding into Dagger Falls, along the Salmon River, through cathedrals of Douglas fir and lodgepole pine. We ate tins of Spam in a meadow. We napped in deep grass while the horses grazed. We made up games in the saddle—*I'll say a word, and you think of a song. Midnight. Midnight Special, CCR. Bird. Blackbird, The Beatles. Boat. Wildflowers, Tom Petty.* And then we'd sing. At night my father shook Jiffy Pop over the fire, and I ate it in my sleeping bag. He told me stories about a haunted barn in Upstate New York. About a bird man who lived in its rafters. I fell asleep thrilled and wasted from sun and riding.

In the morning we saddled our mares and set out for deer.

Holding the pack mule's lead line with one hand and his rifle in the other, my father left the reins draped on the saddle's horn. Quincy led. She was a horse he had bought for cheap, and she fought going into the trailer, fought coming out, sidestepped when saddled, nipped when harnessed. She spooked at fallen tarp or loose bailing twine. She was a real loose cannon.

My father left the reins slack in his lap. We rode through meadows and ravines, down saddles and up ridges. We came to the Salmon River, and Quincy stiffened. He nudged her flank. She tossed her head. Her ears flattened.

"Take Misty in first. Quincy will follow," my father said.

The water rumbled. I dug my heel to her side. She eased her way past the banks, her hooves slipping on mossed rocks. The river ran fast. Misty trudged along. My father bent to Quincy, commanded her into the river. I heard the splash of a horse breaking current; she followed.

The string of horses lunged through the water. Finally, Misty's feet steadied in the river shallows. I heard Quincy's hooves clash on river rock. She broke out of the river and trotted up the bank. We let them rest and graze. We stroked their necks.

The afternoon sun dried our jeans, our saddles. The horses broke sweats, their coats lathered and sweet smelling. Quincy took the lead again, my father still pulling the pack mule, still clutching his rifle, the reins still dangling on the saddle's horn. The forest thinned. We came to a meadow clearing, nothing but bluegrass and wildflowers. Quincy sidestepped. Her croup quivered, her muscles tensed. She spun. She reared up. My father, his steering hand holding his rifle, couldn't reach the reins. She reared up again. Then she threw her head down and bucked, her hind legs straight above her. My father flew from the saddle. I saw him hung in midair, the lead line loosening from his grip but the rifle still in his hand, waving above his head. He crashed onto the saddle horn. His left leg slipped through the stirrup, and when he fell to the ground, his foot stayed caught. Quincy dragged him through dirt and grass. She ran him to the other end of the meadow. Finally, he kicked his foot free and lay in the dirt, the rifle beside him.

I rode to my father. The mule had bolted. Quincy grazed, calm now. He lay on the ground, moving only his head.

My mother says I found the mule, that I rode through the hills and caught her and loaded the horses and broke camp, but I don't remember that.[2] I know the mule came back to us, and the day faded into dusk, and camp was a long ride away. It wasn't the miles of trail that worried me but that icy, fast river. My father walked when he could, and when he couldn't, he lay in the grass, like a dead man in a western. At the river he somehow pulled himself over the saddle and tightened his hold. I sent Misty into the water, pulling the mule behind me, and Quincy followed, obedient now, good now. I turned in my saddle and watched her come through. With each fall of her hoof, I remembered how she'd snorted and kicked, how she'd sent my father flying, with that rifle high above his head.

I never knew what spooked her. There was no trail marker or discarded beer can. Nothing new or unsettling. My father had coaxed her through the river, and it had done no good. The fall broke his pelvis. For weeks he lay on the couch, bags of ice pressed to his lap, and each time I saw him laid out in the living room, that image surfaced: Quincy leaping wildly, the reins just out of reach, that rifle waving.

It was a bad first trip, clearly. Quincy could have dragged him over a rock or felled tree; he could have concussed, bled internally; he could have ruptured a vital organ. And the whole trip seemed pointless. My siblings and I ate my father's venison only under great protest, and we always had a freezer well stocked with Lean Cuisines and store-bought beef patties. Hunting was a sport, his gun a toy. The whole trip was unnecessary.

But I know necessity has no bearing here. I know we are people who enjoy the idea of adversity. We like to think we are tough folks doing tough work—like the cowboys pushing their herd, the homesteaders bringing water to the desert. I see our tendency to hardship, on doing things the uphill way.

But more than any of that, I hated the idea of drawing a bead on a deer; pulling the trigger; watching it bend, then collapse; tugging the liver, the lungs, the heart, from the still-warm body. And mostly I hated that had my father left the gun at camp, he would have held the reins, would have spun Quincy into submission. I pictured that rifle still with him as he lay in the dirt.

My Daisy went untouched. The pop of a yanked trigger, the chill of a steel barrel, was no longer enchanting. The gun didn't conjure the smoking barrels of my Wild West heroes. Now guns seemed hazardous, dangerous, a risk not worth taking.

In some ways Idaho remains an Old West holdout. That herd of mustangs still stampedes the Owyhees; elk and mountain lions scale the Sawtooths. Hills are littered with leaning ghost towns. Their mining shafts are long empty, but the old saloons slant on as monument. If we ignore the suburban Treasure Valley—which covers only about 15 percent of the state's area but is home to almost 60 percent of the population—the state is full of farm towns and brush plains. With our collective insistence on restricted government, Idaho legislation remains nearly the most limited in the nation, a figment of the lawless West. I think of how Cassidy rode into Idaho to rob his bank and then fled back to Wyoming once his lawlessness was done. Modern outlaws know this, and Idaho is home to the last remnant of gunslingers, men who live in Earp and Cassidy's shadows.

In the early 1980s Claude Dallas rolled into the desert, rifle level in his lap. Ohio-born, Dallas was a western dreamer. He longed to live on the prairie, and when the Vietnam War called his name, he hid in southeastern Idaho. He camped along the Owyhee River and allegedly poached bobcats. He ate their meat, wore their skins. He slept beneath the desert stars with nothing but a hide beneath his head and a rifle by his side.

Eventually, the Idaho Department of Fish and Game learned Dallas was illegally killing the big cats. Two officers, Conley Elms and Bill Pogue, drove to Dallas's camp. Dallas saw stirred dust, heard rubber on gravel. He shoved bullets in his .22 and snapped the barrel into place. Dallas fired twice. The men fell. The gun smoked.

Dallas ran. Signs were posted all over town, flashed on local news channels: "Claude Dallas: Wanted. $20,000." Elms's body washed to shore on the banks of the Owyhee River. Dallas kept running.

A year later Dallas was captured and then tried in Caldwell (the courthouse just five minutes from where those few ranchers bid on cattle at the TVLA). Crowds flooded the courtroom. Men wore dusters, black boots, cowboy hats. They slung on holsters heavy with pistols. Women dabbed perfume on their wrists and unbuttoned their pearl-snap blouses. They crashed the courthouse steps, waving signs and blowing kisses, waiting to catch a peek of the outlaw. They called themselves the "Dallas Cheerleaders."

As a kid a decade later, I would hear about Dallas (who is something of a Treasure Valley legend) and think of my old outlaws, the men whose law resistance I had imagined and re-created. I thought of shooting out windshields on Misty's back, pretending I was Cassidy, my pockets weighty with gold. If Dallas was just another western outlaw, hiding in the desert and living by his own rules, then drawing a gun and pulling a trigger seemed violent, vulgar. The whole scenario repulsed me.

When the judge sentenced Dallas to a thirty-year prison term, locals were outraged; thirty years was too harsh for a man brave enough to buck the law. A mob snuck onto the judge's property, shot his German shepherd, and strung it from his front yard maple.

Five years into his term, Dallas smuggled wire cutters into the state penitentiary and clipped his way free—though it's rumored prison guards slipped him the clippers and turned away while he cut through the fence. Idaho natives envisioned him riding into an Owyhee sunset and fanned out hard. A year later police captured Dallas in California and sent him back to the Idaho state pen. Prison officials overlooked the escape. In 2005 he was released early, twenty-two years into his thirty-year term. He left the prison a hero and, rumor has it, moved to Emmett, a town lined with apple orchards. If true, the outlaw's home sits just twenty minutes from Eagle's topiaried lawns and aerobicizing housewives.

Not even a decade after Dallas shot those officers, another outlaw claimed Idaho as home. Ruby Ridge is a patch of blue forest in the northernmost corner of the state. Just forty miles from Canada, the area is dense and remote. In those cutoff mountains, the Aryan Nation set up headquarters. From the mid-1970s to 2001 one of the oldest and most extreme neo-Nazi outposts camped out (for a long time Idaho was known for the white supremacists and potato farms and little more; how embarrassing). Randy Weaver, a sergeant Green Beret, and radical fundamentalist, moved his family from the Midwest and settled in those mountains. Stricken with delusions of apocalypse, Weaver and his wife, Vicki, hoped the isolation would prove a haven when civilization ended.

Inevitably, Weaver crossed paths with the Aryan Nation. An antigovernment zealot, Weaver shrugged off the few gun laws Idaho enforces (so few, in fact, that Idaho is second only to Arizona for having the most permissive gun laws in the United States) and sold illegal firearms to the white supremacists. Soon enough, an undercover officer caught Weaver sawing off shotguns and selling them to the neo-Nazis.

Weaver was subpoenaed for illegally selling firearms. Dismissive of the government as ever, he failed to show up in court. In an effort to track his activity and ensure he wasn't providing weapons for an Aryan militia, U.S. marshals surveilled the Weaver property.

The details of the event now famously known as the Standoff at Ruby Ridge are hazy. We know that in the late summer of 1992 two marshals walked onto Weaver's land. Weaver's hounds, sniffing a strange scent from the dirt path, howled. His son, fourteen-year-old Sammy, knew the dogs' barks meant visitors. He lit down the mountain path, a .22 rifle in arm. What transpired is unclear, but someone raised a gun to his cheek and squeezed a trigger, that first shot fired. Rifles cracked. Bullets flew. Sammy was shot dead. More marshals were called in. Weaver gathered his family—two teenage daughters, his wife, and a baby girl—and barricaded them in the cabin. Each woman lay on the ground, keeping her head low, her gun pressed to her chest. Four hundred marshals surrounded the property. They staked out in the forest, tried to get a bead on Weaver's back. A day passed. No one moved in the Weaver home. Three hundred FBI flew in. Helicopters circled overhead. Armed federal agents blocked the bridge to the Weaver property—a war zone, a showdown.

Idahoans, still crushing on outlaws, rallied in the woods and pitched protest signs against the police. Folk artists wrote songs in support of Weaver and sang their ballads from the pines.

Finally, the cabin door opened. It's assumed Vicki Weaver was going to try to gather her son's body. When an antsy sniper fired, Vicki was killed, her baby crying in her arms. The marshals called for surrender; again, Weaver refused. Another day passed. Another. Weaver ventured from his cabin once, to bring in Sammy's body. The marshals shot his arm. His daughter made him a tourniquet, and he stayed locked in his home, shotgun snug at his side.

My family watched the FBI storm the forest on television. The myth—safe in its distance—had morphed into reality. The heroes of my youth transformed. No more BBs and Coke cans, now shotguns and buckshot. Every night we turned on the news and watched the standoff, the SWAT team circled and ready, waiting to fire. Neighbors sat on our couch, jaw-dropped at the footage. "Damn government," they would say. "Man's just trying to live"—that familiar disdain. But Weaver had sawed off shotguns and tried to sell them to white supremacists—no small transgression. "Can't kill a man for protecting his family," they would say. And this I tried to understand. His son was dead, his wife too. Maybe it was sloppy police work. But he could have lowered his rifle, could have taken the guns from his daughters' chests.

Ten days passed. With half his family dead and his wound infecting, he stumbled from his cabin, his gun raised above his head.

Richfield is a dusty town in the desert of southeastern Idaho, and for sixty years the locals have celebrated Outlaw Day by dressing as their favorite lawbreakers, Cassidy or Sundance, Dallas or Weaver. They gallop their horses through Main Street, reenacting bank robberies and gunfights, and I think, as a girl, I would have loved this. Would have loved the smell of oiled saddles, loved watching the horses rear and spin, loved the blast of fresh buckshot. I would have reimagined those Old West heroes drawing quick and shooting fast. But after Dallas and Weaver, after my father's hard fall, I could not imagine watching in awe as the locals galloped their geldings through town, as they blasted gunpowder into a late-summer sky.

By thirteen, just on the other side of childhood, I'd outgrown my gun. These criminals outshined the gunslingers of my youth. Dallas and Weaver were an embarrassment. To the rest of America, Idaho was a land full of anti-government zealots and lunatic bobcat poachers, an anarchy ruled by gun-toting crazy men.

With Dallas allegedly living in the next town over and Weaver a statewide hero, I became a Democrat and preached about government intervention and gun control. I hid my Daisy in the garage behind shovels and fishing poles.

In the gun and the outlaw, I see the most intact threads of this old story. To say Idaho is still a land of gunslingers doesn't seem like a stretch. Consult the bumper stickers and voting polls. Idahoans fight for their guns. We pack heat always. We cheer for Dallas and Weaver and revere criminality and violence. One hundred years ago Wyatt and Butch, now Dallas and Weaver. For once so little has changed. This part of the old model is alive and well. And what a tragic inversion it is. For all the romantic, lovely threads of this story that are outdated (the mint fields, the horse fields, the mustangs, the cowboys), that demand to be replaced, to be evolved out of, the shoot-'em-up heroes charge on. They are healthy and thriving, offering little opportunity to leave them behind and find something new, something different, something civil and humane. Here we have a moment of myth preserved, of myth gruesome in its reality.

The year I left for college, my father purchased a handgun for my sister. "For when you're on campus at night," he told her, referring to her night classes at Boise State University, which is as crime free as Boise itself, a city with 60 percent fewer instances of violent crime than the national average. She turned the handgun over in her palm, steely and shining. She packed her gun to work, to dinner, on dates; on her lunch break she went to a shooting range and practiced. I found it unnecessary and off-putting. I came home from Boston for Christmas break, and he offered to buy me a pistol too.

"You can never be too safe," he said. Massachusetts has strict gun control laws. Even Mace sales are regulated. I couldn't imagine Bostonians cheering on Claude Dallas or Randy Weaver. I was a world away from the lawless West.

"No thanks," I told him.

"But what if I get you one anyway?" he asked.

"I'll return it."

In my father's desire for us to pack heat, I see an echo of Weaver barricaded in his cabin, each of his remaining kids aiming her gun. Both men wanted daughters who knew how to load and fire, how to protect themselves. The intention, I suppose, is not a bad one.

But I'm stuck on what compelled them. Weaver had that apocalyptic delusion; my father feared for our safety in a sleepy, low-crime city. Maybe living inside a tradition that says *Shit can go sideways, better be prepared* breeds a paranoia and defensiveness that doesn't serve us well.

While living back east, I'd make weekend treks to my grandparents' cabin in Upstate New York, those hills near where my father grew up. Just inside the Adirondacks, I'd stop in a paint-peeled gas station. Eventually, the owner—the only person ever manning the register—and I became friendly. "Where you from?" the clerk asked.

"Idaho."

"Randy Weaver country," he said. "I met him once. A goddamn hero."

For once I said *Idaho* and someone knew where I was talking about. I took my change and walked out the door.

When I left Boston, I returned to the same boyfriend I'd had for years, that alfalfa farmer whose sister-in-law held four rodeo queen titles. In him I saw myself in sharp relief. Like Mary Clearman Blew and William Kittredge, he was a traditional westerner. He grew up on a real farm, learned to drive a tractor before a car, and had a brother who team roped. And I was his "Eagle girlfriend," as his family described me, whose parents had eastern accents.

Wes Lexley Ford is the largest car dealership in the Treasure Valley, which is to say the largest in Idaho. My boyfriend washed cars at the dealership, and each summer the company rented a golf course and hosted a picnic. It would be catered. There would be raffles. There were worse ways to spend an afternoon.

Planning on driving the golf cart and avoiding a five iron at all costs, I wore a starched summer dress and spiked heels. At hole nine a pair of men blocked the tee. Their dusters flapped in a hot wind, their boots filmed with dust, their shotguns crooked in their arms. They looked like Blondie or Wyatt or Butch. They squinted into the sun. The company had surprised its employees with a clay pigeon stand, and the workers loved it.

My boyfriend leaped from the golf cart and raised the gun to his cheek. "Pull," he yelled, that familiar command. A pigeon soared through the sky. Three times he fired, and three times the discs erupted. He stretched the gun to me.

"No thanks."

"Come on," he said. I refused; he insisted.

Maybe trying to live down my Eagle stigma, I wobbled to the shotgun, my stilettos sinking in the grass. Smooth and polished, it was just like the gun Alex had used in the desert a decade earlier. I hadn't fired a gun in years. I raised the butt to my shoulder, felt the oil on my cheek, the wood rubbed smooth, the dusty smell of fired shots. I worried the rifle would smudge dirt into my dress. I remembered the skin beat tender from the shotgun's kickback; I remembered all those staring boys, the thud of a pigeon missed. I pictured little Sammy Weaver, his .22 bobbing as he ran down the path. "Pull," I said. I closed both eyes. I saw my father flung from his saddle, his rifle waving over his head. I pulled the trigger, and somewhere, far beyond the bluffs, I shot a hole in the sky.

The shooting range is nearly empty. In the front of the store it is just the salesman and me.

"Lots of people come in curious," he tells me. "I usually let them shoot something like this." He taps the mammoth pistol at his waist. "They don't come back after that." He lets out a startlingly high-pitched laugh.

In the fifteen years since I opened that Daisy, I have become increasingly concerned about our collective attachment to the gun. Americans own more guns, per capita, than residents in any other country. The United States is home to less than 5 percent of the world's population, but we experience over 30 percent of global mass shootings. Just three years after I got my air rifle, the Columbine Massacre stripped away the sense of security and safety children assumed in a classroom. My niece, when she goes to kindergarten, will be asked to imagine a person firing a gun at her, shooting to kill. She will be told to hide behind her desk or run serpentine for the door or jump out a window. Americans shoot up school cafeterias and synagogues and mosques and black churches and movie theaters. In my lifetime America has seen over 110 gun massacres. This is nothing short of fucked-up.

I want to tell the man at the counter that I am not curious about buying a gun. I am not curious if I will feel safer with it riding heavy in my purse. I am curious, I should say, about what it will feel like now to pick one up and lay heavy on the trigger. I am curious if I can pull it back at all.

I haven't shot a gun since that wasted shot on the golf course. Six years later I feel displaced, disconnected from my roots. I feel like that college freshman, barefoot in Boston. In Idaho I am a big-government sucker, a yuppie liberal who grows uneasy around the things that grew me: pistols crossed above fireplaces, closets cluttered with rifles. To the rest of the world, I am a girl raised to load and shoot a rifle. Maybe, somehow, the pop of a spent shell is still satisfying. Maybe I will take aim and only remember those long afternoons spent horseback in Eagle's hills with nothing but the sounds of my mare breaking through dried sage and the ping of a hit target. I am curious to see if that woman on the golf course still exists, that girl in her sharp heels and silk ruffles, taking aim and hitting nothing. I am curious to see which of these women I have become.

You can't escape where you come from; you can't run from yourself; you can take the girl out of the country, but you can't take the country out of the girl—all those cornball truisms and country song lyrics. But I'd shelved my Daisy, had refused my father's pistol. In so many ways I have felt like a stranger to these parts. I remember the girl packing heat, albeit BB gun heat, on her horse, and I barely recognize her. Yet here I stand, eyeing a case of guns.

Today is a clear, summer day—my friends are already at the park playing bocce ball and passing iced tea; my sister and her daughter skip rocks at the river's shore; my mother is home roasting a chicken. If I were in Tucson, Ryan and I would be on our back stoop, reading in the shade, drinking cold beers because in that kind of heat, it's never too early for a Corona. Instead, I am standing with the salesman in his bulging jeans, and I am trying to choose my weapon. I look at the hanging shotguns and think of the dangers of a story that so deeply reveres lawlessness, a story that tells us we can shoot up whomever we like whenever because this is the West and we're tough sons-of-guns. I think of the romanticism, turned vulgar, that keeps us charmed by lawlessness, that drives us to cheer on killers. I get all that, and I don't like it one bit.

But beneath all my objections and self-consciousness and nerves, a current of adrenaline pulses. I am equal parts terrified and thrilled, and there's something else too, something I can't account for; call it memory (nostalgia? romance still?). I recall my Daisy, its chintzy plastic body and thin barrel and wheezing fire; I see my father tucking the gun to my shoulder for the first time; I hear the pop of my first target hit. In this moment, with the salesman waiting for me to name my game, that impulse to flatly reject this narrative dies down. To blatantly refuse the gun—to say I cannot rent a .22 to shoot for sport in a range—feels as unreasonable as unquestionably loving it, and I wonder if I should quit these binaries, the harsh extremes of acceptance versus rejection, and instead strive for some sort of in-between, to balance the beauty and the disgust, the magnificence and the rats, as Emerson says.

It is Ladies' Night at the Marksman Pistol Range. Of course it is. Westerners are fixated with chicks and pistols. Annie Oakley, my sister, the Weaver girls, those rodeo queens dancing in their leather gowns, teeny revolvers strapped to their thighs. All those women proudly packing, and here a whole night devoted to gals and Glocks. In this collision I see another iteration of our infatuation with toughness, even (especially) in women. But with the exception of one woman, a stooped seventy-year-old firing a colossal handgun, I am the only lady in sight.

"Experience level?" the salesman asks.

"None." And this feels true.

"What you want to shoot?"

I look into the case. A million black pistols spoon each other. Bigger and smaller variations of the same thing. I do not know their names. I can tell a revolver from an automatic, a pistol from a rifle, and beyond that, I am lost. The walls are draped with shotguns and rifles. Boxes of bullets and shells are stacked in cabinets. The aisles are cluttered with trash bins full of discarded shells, gold and shining, empty husks. In every corner a gun case glows, pistols on display. It smells like dirt and grease. I remember that first shotgun fired, that unsteadying kickback.

"Nothing big," I say.

He hands me a .22 semiautomatic. "Magazine here. Safety there. Don't shoot me." That is all the training he will give. Just like that, he extends the gun to me. It is black, dull, ugly. My chest tightens. The building is one big room; a glass wall divides it into two halves. The front half is the store, guns for sale, a cash register, a place to buy a target. On the other side of the glass sits the range: ten booths lined up, like a bowling alley; partitions separating cubbies; a little counter to rest the gun.

"Will you carry it in?" I ask. He rolls his eyes and walks me to the other side of the glass wall. My cubby is next to the granny's. He clips on my target. "Better start at nine feet." He flicks a switch, and the target scoots down the lane.

"Before I forget, you turn around with that gun in your hand, you're gonna have my rifle pointing back. And my aim is good."

I nod in agreement, and he leaves me alone with the pistol. I roll my shoulders, try to steady my breathing. I stare at the gun. I feel woozy. The granny next to me fires. Even through my earmuffs the blast is huge. I jump. She fires again, a quick succession. Her target waves on impact. The blasts erupt in my chest.

I pick up the gun. It is cold in my hands. I drop the bullets into the magazine, click it into place. I raise the pistol. Maybe I will feel eight years old again, leveling my sights in my BB gun, my father commanding, "Squint that eye. Breathe deep. Ease into the trigger." Maybe I will squint and breathe and ease and the gun will kick in my hand. The jolt will be gentler than the shotguns, but I will still be surprised at the great charge through my wrist, up my arm. I will bring in my target. One dark bead in the forehead. *A sure shot.* The woman beside me will fire again, her gun booming into rhythm, her shells flying. I will move the target out another ten feet, will aim, squint, breathe, ease. A hole to the chest. At thirty feet I'll fire again. For a split second those outlaws I have grown ashamed of will be a world away, Dallas and Weaver forgotten in their gross and mythic fame. I will not think of the lawmen falling dead. I will not think of the rifle barrels pointing from cabin windows. They will be there but, for a moment, forgotten. I will hear the granny's gun, the basso rhythm bang, my gun's higher, quicker ping. They will fire and boom. A rhythm, an orchestra. My pulse will pound with their beat. I will send the target down the lane, seventy-five feet out, as far as the range permits. I will riddle the target's chest, its head. Shells will fire fast, one after the other. They will fly from the gun like sparks, like confetti, like hail. I will be Annie on a stallion, blowing apples to bits. I will be Blondie busting my pistol from my hip. I will be alone in a hayfield, my finger heavy on the trigger, the high tinkle of a windshield shattered. Misty will shift at the rifle's fire, and I'll raise the gun again.

But this does not happen.

I raise the gun. I pull the trigger. My arm jumps. The hot shell bursts from the pistol and rolls down my shirt. How quickly the skin blisters into a crescent welt. There is my father flung from his horse, there is Sammy Weaver dropped dead. There is my target, in the shape of a man, with a hole in its chest. My palms beat hot and wet. Whatever balance I had hoped to strike—to love this in the right way—I realize is impossible. The repulsion outweighs the affection. No beauty, all disgust. Any attachment I might have harbored feels trivial and self-indulgent. A frivolity demanded in exchange for very real violence. The granny reloads and fires on. I put the gun down.

I still have to pay the man.

"Looks like you've got the better part of a round to finish," he says, dismantling the .22.

"Just close me out," I say.

"Want your target?"

But before I can answer, I am already gone.

True Grit, Country Strong, and Other Lies

My last day in Eagle is quiet. Before my flight I sit on the porch and drink coffee and watch my father move irrigation lines from one ditch to another. A gelding paces in the corral and a Hereford grazes, and on the other side of the fence, my niece splashes in sprinklers. A lone jogger laps Rio Bellisimo's empty sidewalks. I've had a proper Idaho summer: barbecues and rodeos and the state fair. I've bought linen sundresses and huarache sandals and gorged on banh mi sandwiches and those heavily frosted cupcakes, and now I am ready to leave. Eagle's boutiques close at six, and the restaurants are overtaken by off-key jazz quartets. (Ryan says Eagle's bar scene, with all those upper-middle-class white folks grooving to Sinatra covers, looks like the outtakes for a Cialis commercial.) When my parents drive me to the airport, there is no teary good-bye, no worrying about being able to settle back in Arizona, no wondering if I'll be able to stay gone.

As the plane lifts, I do not watch the foothills broaden beneath me. Instead, I set my seat back and close my eyes and think of my and Ryan's bed, how in the winter we sleep with the windows open and the night smells like eucalyptus and orange blossoms.

In Tucson the heat is unbearable (stepping off the plane, my bare shoulders sting in the sun), but I'd missed the eggs benedicts and tequila sunrises I make with Ryan, the acacia trees in our yard, our evening walks through Tucson's palm-lined, stucco neighborhoods, the houses a wash of bright blues, deep corals. I arrive early in the evening and am relieved to be back. This has been the longest stretch Ryan and I have gone without seeing each other. I ride beside him in our pickup and keep my head on his shoulder until we are home. We drop off my luggage and go, as we so often do, for a walk. Fourth Avenue is alive with drum circles and hipsters on bicycles and dogs chained to benches. Every bar's crowd spills onto the sidewalk, where the air at least moves. We eat beef tortas in the street. We are sweaty. We are tired. It is late. But instead of heading home, we drive to the movie theater (plush seats, an iced cola, air conditioning), and I have the new Coen brothers' film *True Grit* on the mind.

The film, an adaptation of the Charles Portis novel of the same name, tells the story of the sharp-witted, tough-as-nails, pious Mattie Ross and her quest to avenge her father's death. When the film premiered, the critics freaked (favorably), and in its first month it grossed more money than any other Coen brothers film (which includes cult favorites such as *Fargo*, *The Big Lebowski*, and Academy Award winner *No Country for Old Men*). As if I needed any more nudging, friends—typically of Idaho origin—relished in its westernness.

I'd already seen it in Eagle, twice, but now—like any hardcore fan—I have to show Ryan. But we are too late; the last showing started twenty minutes ago. We scan the marquis, and in fifteen minutes *Country Strong* begins. Garnering much less critical praise and barely turning a profit at the box office, the movie stars Gwyneth Paltrow in her first lead role since who knows when. The actress gained an undetectable-yet-much-hyped twelve pounds, forced a lilting southern accent, donned a silver cross necklace, and boot-scooted onto the screen as Kelly Canter, a rehabbing country pop singer trying to manage her personal life and career. Admittedly, I could claim we'd chosen the movie blindly. And while this is sort of true, there's more to it than that. A small part of me was intrigued by Shana Feste's country star saga. It echoes my fascination with

Lady Antebellum: here another mainstream representation of "country," and I am curious to see how it is defined and handled. What's more, Gwyneth–turned–Kelly Canter, in her bouffant and jean jacket, tapped into my guilty pleasure zone. In this film I'd get to indulge in the vision of the West I've so loved: dirty bars, pastel prairies, cracked boots, whiny singers. Gwyneth, with her (sort of) Texan accent, glittered cheeks, and enormous hair, reminded me of those western women who populate the small towns of Idaho, the ranchers' wives, the rodeo queens. Thus, bucking all my better judgment, I watch the thing.

All this is not to suggest that I am merely intrigued by the fact that I watched each of these films, though that might merit some consideration (especially in *Country Strong's* case). What I want to consider most is that each film offers an explanation of what it means to be a western woman, and in this consideration I am transfixed.

Women in the West have their own mythology, and it is one I've never necessarily settled into. The most foreboding figure, in my imagination, has been Ma Ingalls: the silent, butter-churning mother who nursed scarlet fever from her children; the wife who gauzed her husband's cuts. She is strong, sure, but her strength is, notably, second to her sweetness. In the face of blizzard and drought, ruined crops and empty grain bins, all of her husband's business struggles, she remains cheery. Even more emblazoned in my mind is Laura, the sweet and spunky (again, sweetness before spunk) wholesome daughter who adores her father and respects her mother, whose only dream is to stay on the prairie, marry a farm boy, run a schoolhouse, and rear some babies (that I, like my sister and every other girl I grew up with, read all the *Little House* books should shock no one—it was what we girls did).

While the mythology remains thin (and oh so sweet), the more honest story of Old West women is difficult to fit into this idealized, clean-scrubbed version. The earliest frontierswomen, we know, were generally prostitutes. Often no older than thirteen, they struggled to make it in a land shaped by the mining, farming, and ranching industries. A tough land full of tough work for tough men. In the story of the West we tell to young girls, the floozies have no place. Thus, enter the Ingalls women, those sweetheart pioneers. Women so mild and pure, who never shot a gun or disagreed with a man or lost their tempers—I rarely related to them. I watched Ma and sister Mary and, in her less spunky moments, Laura and was, to be honest, bored.

Not only were the Ingalls boring, had Ma Ingalls really existed, she likely would have met the fate of so many pioneer women: depression, laudanum addiction, psychosis.[1] Long winters shut in on the frozen prairies drove women mad. Wives, stuck indoors as their husbands hunted or trapped or mined, would grow so desperate for conversation they would keep a caged canary in their home, its sharp song the only voice beside their own.

I have looked at these women, and I am left wanting. The prostitutes and forced shut-ins and the few who prevailed (but their stories are seldom told) have never entered into my vision of this place. So I have turned to these two films hoping to find a western woman who looks like someone I might recognize or someone I might hope to see.

I shall admit that *True Grit* I have loved and *Country Strong* I have hated. I was so charmed by *True Grit* that I saw it twice in one week, read the book, saw it again, and then watched the John Wayne original. *Country Strong*, however, was entertaining, sure, but not in any of its intended ways. I laughed when my fellow cinema patrons cried and cried (nearly) when they laughed. I realize emotional proclamations such as these deserve explanation, so let us consider first how the two films differ. The Academy darling, can-do-no-wrong Coen brothers (exempting that whole *Lady Killers* debacle) have earned nothing but praise with *True Grit*. The *New York Times* rated the film 10/10; *Los Angeles Times*, *Slate*, and the *New Yorker* 9/10. Conversely, the *New York Times* gave *Country Strong* a 5/10, as did the *Los Angeles Times*, and the *New Yorker* (predictably) wouldn't go near the thing.

The disparity here is obvious. *True Grit* is a nearly flawless piece of cinema, while *Country Strong*, to be blunt, is nothing but flawed. To anyone who has seen both films (or even read about them), this is fairly obvious. From the writing to the acting to the cinematography, the films are different creatures. The Coen brothers, who are seasoned screenwriters, wisely lifted the bulk of the film's killer dialogue right from the Portis classic. They enlisted Hollywood's finest actors (Jeff Bridges played Rooster with an unparalleled swagger, and newcomer Hailee Steinfeld blew everyone away with her rigid, hyper-articulated Mattie), and the Coens' old pal, cinematographer Roger Deakins, served up a characteristically visually stunning film.

Conversely, Shana Feste—who has written and directed only one other film, last year's *The Greatest*, which few people saw and even fewer enjoyed—relied on the tabloid stories of Britney Spears for her inspiration (a dubious impetus at best). Gwyneth Paltrow, who often delivers in the acting department, flounders here (but perhaps this is a result of that script—she is asked to cry in nearly each scene and do little more, which leaves her few opportunities to wow us). The rest of the cast is largely populated by teen soap stars (from soaps I admittedly and semi-shamefully love, *Friday Night Lights* and *Gossip Girl*). Real-life country singer Tim McGraw plays Kelly's husband-manager, and while he isn't an absolute flop here, he's certainly better left in a recording studio. Cinematographically, there isn't a single frame of note.

To each of the films' credits, they are different things with different objectives. Not every movie needs to be Oscar material. And certainly *Country Strong* has its place. The theater Ryan and

I attended was packed. When I saw *True Grit*, the theater—one of those small rooms at the end of a hall—was quarter-full. For Kelly Canter more seats and more seats filled.[2] More important, my fellow moviegoers seemed to genuinely like it. They laughed and cried in all the intended places, and even the voices of film criticism weren't always so harsh. *Variety* gave the film a generous 7/10, describing it as "that rare ensemble piece in which all four principals are not only compellingly drawn but handled with an astute sense of dramatic balance." Clearly, not everyone found *Country Strong* to be so weak.

So I am partial, biased, prone to play favorites. I indulged in two films about western women, and I fell hard for one and hated the other. This is the nature of the audience—we are fickle, biased creatures—and that I prefer one film isn't all that monumental. What's more compelling is that each movie has tried to round out the western woman canon (isn't this what I've been after?). And beyond that, both movies are equally concerned with womanhood *and* toughness, that other theme I love so well.

Everywhere I turn, this story declares our toughness: fence cutters battling over property lines; rodeo queens muscling strange horses around corrals; young girls shooting fast and far; men killing game just to prove they can. And these films are no exception. Maybe, then, they are able to offer someone so unlike those tenderhearted Ingalls girls?

As the title suggests, *True Grit* is a story of resolve. But too often—certainly in the John Wayne flick and, occasionally, even in the novel—the audience is led to believe it's Rooster's toughness that matters most. After all, upon first meeting the marshal, fourteen-year-old Mattie says she'd like to employ him because she has heard he is a "man with true grit." But let us not be fooled. Mattie is characterized by nothing more than her hard-bitten-ness. In the wake of her father's murder, she is left to handle the business (her mother is grief-stricken, and she is the eldest of three children—

though I imagine that even if her mother were able, Mattie would have insisted on handling the business of death). After shipping her father's body home, she watches a hanging without flinching and then visits Col. G. Stonehill's stockyard, where her father had boarded his mare and bought a clutter of mustangs. Mattie, in her stubbornness and smarts, convinces Stonehill to buy back the ponies, which she now has no use for. In her hour of grieving, Mattie outsmarts a businessman to the tune of three hundred dollars.

Then, poised as ever, she visits the boardinghouse where her father was staying and collects his belongings. The scene is short— especially given the long, dialogue-riddled scenes the Coens open with—but important. For the first time the audience sees how much her father meant to her. Mattie looks at his things—a coat, a hat, a Colt revolver—and she doesn't cry or wallow, but her face softens and in her eyes there is something tender, like pain, but it lasts only a moment, and the next thing we know she is buying a flour bag from the landlady for toting the gun.

After collecting her father's things, she chases down the sheriff, demanding to know what will come of her father's murderer, Tom Chaney. When she learns that essentially nothing will happen, she asks for the best bounty hunter, and the sheriff advises her to use a man named Quinn, "a good peace officer and a lay preacher to boot . . . He is straight as a string." He goes on to caution "the meanest one is Rooster Cogburn. He is . . . double-tough, and fear don't enter into his thinking." Mattie asks, "Where can I find this Rooster?"

Once she has commissioned the marshal (who had his reservations about working for a child, but—like Stonehill before him—caved to her relentless arguing), Mattie's toughness is really tried. She insists on going into the "wild" Choctaw Nation with Rooster (he balks and assures her "This ain't no coon hunt," but she eventually wears him down). In the Indian Nation (and here comes a spoiler alert, but might I suggest you use this pause as an opportunity to watch the film—only more spoilers will ensue from here), she dodges bullets, cuts a dead man from an oak, watches a man slice off another man's fingers, witnesses numerous murders, finds Tom Chaney and tries to take him at gunpoint (her gun misfires) and is instead abducted. In each situation Mattie proves tougher than the last. Not once does she balk or whine or whimper for home.

While abducted, she really wows us. Not only did she find Tom Chaney and try to arrest him (a normal, less gritty child would have run for Rooster), but she is calm and composed when abducted. All three of the *True Grit* iterations—the Portis novel, the Wayne classic, and now the Coen piece for which I'm so tipsy—vary, but perhaps not in any way more significantly than the manner in which the evil Tom Chaney is taken out. To summarize (big spoiler), Mattie and her captor are in the woods, and she begins—just as she did with the stock keeper and Rooster—to bargain. If he will let her go, she will testify that he released her, thereby lessening his conviction. Chaney instead decides he can silence her himself.

In the novel and in the John Wayne classic, Mattie squeals in terror, and Rooster emerges from the pines and takes out ol' Chaney. But the Coen brothers get it right. Understanding the importance of toughness, especially for our girl Mattie, they do a little rewriting. Here Rooster is still a ways off, battling Lucky Ned in the plains below, and Mattie scrambles for Chaney's rifle. He lunges at her, and she cocks the gun back and fires right into his face. He topples over the ledge, and Mattie the teen has killed her man.

In this moment I am smitten. I watch Mattie take down the bad guy and nearly leap from my seat in applause. A tougher girl (or boy) I've never seen. Mattie cries only once in the film—not after her father's death or after being bitten by a snake and left for dead—but when her trusty horse, Little Blackie, runs so long and so hard it collapses and dies. In the novel Mattie weeps three times (and each time, who could blame her!). In the Wayne film Mattie squeals and cries the whole way through. I cannot help but discuss specifically that scene where the Coen Mattie so tenderly looks over her father's belongings. The moment is subdued and fleeting, and tough Mattie never cracks, but she almost does, and that is enough. The Wayne Mattie, though, holds her father's watch to the light, then rubs it to her cheek and shakes with sobs. Not that we could blame her for this, but grit it does not display.

The Coen bros know that in the western nothing matters more than toughness. We do not want the bounty hunter who is fair and Bible loving and thorough. We want double-tough, mean-as-sin Rooster. And if we have a hero in this film, it's the teen girl who does not weep at her father's death, does not hesitate when the bad man needs shooting.

And now, I promise, all over-the-top proclamations of love shall cease. Let us instead consider that other film I can't shake. If Mattie is a superhero of epic, gritty proportions, then *Country Strong*'s Kelly Canter is a sad, sorry sucker whose greatest vice is her lack of grit. A cautionary tale of drunkenness and demise, the film offers an example of what we mustn't become. Kelly is clearly a woman—a product—handled by her husband-manager. The film begins with Kelly in rehab. She has just miscarried—a by-product of drinking and gestating—and is now trying to get clean. The husband-manager announces that she'll begin touring again, and we sense that Kelly doesn't want to go, that she isn't confident in her recovery, yet she packs her bags and follows him to the limo, bleary-eyed and shuffling. Where Mattie would have bartered and argued, Kelly weeps a little and nods in compliance.

Never once does Kelly assert herself. In fact, she doesn't really do much at all besides drink, have sex, and cry . . . a lot. And this is no exaggeration. The *New York Times* review of the film—which is a reaming—is titled, "I Am Woman, Hear Me Sob Y'all." Always Kelly is crying, typically without specified cause. The audience doesn't even see her struggle with the addiction. She is just addicted, without any hope of recovery.

Her lack of toughness isn't the only way Shana engages this theme. Most obviously, consider the film's title, *Country Strong*. I confess, I am not entirely sure I understand the phrase. What is meant by *country*? Does Shana mean to say *rural*? Or *this nation*? And what about whatever she's referring to is particularly strong? At first glance the term—familiar in its western, boot-up-yer-ass rhetoric—is passable, but after closer examination, I'm perplexed as to what the words actually mean. Confusing as it is, the film's name is also the title of Kelly Canter's biggest hit single, which essentially delivers the entire mythos of western hardness in two verses and a chorus. The lyrics paint harsh land, people of faith, people who fight (if provoked), but mostly, people who rise up and soldier on. Of course, the great irony is that Kelly isn't country strong. All of the dramatic tension in *Country Strong* boils down to this: Will Kelly toughen up? Just before the film's climax, in a conversation between Kelly's husband and her boyfriend, an aspiring country singer she met in rehab, the husband professes, "Man, she used to be tough as nails." The boyfriend asks, "What happened?" and—in one of the film's many failings—the husband replies, with a shrug, "I don't know." The film is cuing in its audience that at the heart of Kelly's undoing lies her inability to get gritty. Her resolve has left her, and now she is shorn Samson. Without her toughness she is nothing.

The same dramatic question (the film's only dramatic question, really—will Kelly get tough?) drives the rest of the movie. She has three concerts scheduled, three opportunities to get clean and back on track. Predictably, she fails the first two—at her first concert she goes onstage hammered and cries into the microphone, à la Amy Winehouse near the end, and is ushered offstage. The second time she fails to show at all (she is passed out in a car). By the third concert, everything is on the line. If she blows this opportunity, the industry—embodied by a man who schedules her shows

(I was never clear on his title, agent maybe?)—will walk out on her. Can she rise above? Can she muster the strength to make it through her set? Can she beat the addiction? And the film seems to conflate these two issues, leading the audience to believe that if she can only perform well, all else will be solved.

The big night arrives, and she goes onstage, and the melody to "Country Strong" cues, and Kelly's chin quivers; her eyes dart. She strums limply and stares into the mic. She sings the verse diffidently at first, but then, as the music crescendos, her confidence builds. At the chorus she belts out *Country strong!* and her arm shoots into the air above her. The next ten minutes are a music video montage. She boot scoots and drops it like it's hot—though it should be noted that Gwyneth could have spent more time at country pop concerts to see how Hillary Scott and Faith Hill really dance; too often, she swiveled her severely yoga-ed legs like the wife of Chris Martin at Coachella, a little too hip, a little too smooth. A real diva, she changes wardrobes. She wears tight shorts and short skirts and a ball gown flanked in sequins. She closes the concert with a sweet song about going home, while footage of a young Kelly Canter blowing out birthday candles rolls. The crowd goes nuts. She looks out at them, assaulted by that spotlight, and smiles weakly. Offstage she takes a deep breath, her eyes water, and she locks herself in her dressing room.

The husband-manager and boyfriend-singer jump for joy. Kelly is back. She has toughened up. She could muster through one good concert, and they are all on their way again. Champagne corks fly. Of course, the audience remembers the locked door, the ominous look on sad Kelly's face. And when the boyfriend knocks at her door, then pounds, then kicks it in, we are not surprised to see her lifeless—head lolled, legs spread—on the couch, an empty bottle of pills at her side. (No apologies on this spoiler as I have zero reverence for the film and would strongly urge you to avoid it. Now that I've spoiled the ending, you have no incentive, I promise.)

The film feels like a fairy tale, like Red Riding Hood cautioning us from straying into the woods, except here we are reminded to stay tough, to never lose our resolve. For if we are weak, we just might end up collapsed in a green room, our extramarital boyfriend–cowboy–crooner weeping at our side.

Say what I may about either of these films, I must acknowledge that they both struck a nerve. They both offered portrayals of tough or once tough western women, and isn't that what I'd asked for? That I am not ambivalent about either seems important. Sure, *True Grit* was a fine film, but haven't I been excessive? I rarely see films in the theater, and to see one film twice and to read the book and to watch the John Wayne original—admittedly, I did so that I might fall even deeper in love with the Coens' piece, so I could know my boys had done it best—isn't it all a bit much? And finer films have been made; nobody's calling this the next *Citizen Kane*. Furthermore, I would never argue that it's spotless. I take issue with the framing technique of both the Coen film and the novel. What is charming in Mattie as a fourteen-year-old—her , stubbornness and piety—is less charming in Mattie as an adult, and therefore I do not delight in her narration. And there have arguably been better films this year; though *True Grit* was nominated for ten Academy Awards, it won zero. But I am lovestruck. Say what you will of the film's artistic quality (which is grade A), mostly I am smitten because Mattie is one tough badass. When I see her, I like to think that someday I could abide shootouts and snakebites all in the name of vengeance. Of course, a less true thing could never be uttered. I could hardly lie in a den of rattlesnakes and not pass out from fear. I nearly trembled just watching it.

And what of *Country Strong*? It was bad, most everyone agrees, but it wasn't the worst film I've ever seen . . . not even from Gwyneth. (Remember *Shallow Hal*? A special kind of bad.) In fact, in film critics' worst-films-of-the-year lists, *Country Strong* was only mentioned by *Rolling Stone*. What's more, *Entertainment Weekly* compiled critic reviews, and both films received a B rating—*True Grit* a plus and *Country Strong* a minus, but still, they're in the same family. Yet I have railed against it to everyone I know, cautioning them away from it as though watching the thing would infect them with disease. Warranted or not, each of these films has planted in me a full-on, deep-seated obsession, an obsession I know has to do with the films' discourses on femininity and toughness.

Just as I love *True Grit* not for its cinematography or acting but, ultimately, for Mattie's toughness, my disdain for *Country Strong* has less to do with the shoddy script and flat acting and more to do with sad, weak Kelly. What I buck so hard against in *Country Strong* is that we have a story of a woman lying down and quitting. She doesn't put up a fight or try hard. She just cries and whines and dies. And if I have found a western model in Mattie, then in Kelly I see not only another discard-able western female prototype but one that is particularly grating. Worse than the too-sweet Ingalls is weak-willed Kelly. Nothing irritates me more than watching Kelly cry. Kelly onstage, crying. Kelly in her dressing room, crying. Kelly crying quietly in the back of a limo. Kelly sobbing into her boyfriend's shoulder. And maybe it's the frequency that frustrates me or the fact that I seldom understand *why* she's crying, or maybe (and here, I sense, is the real ticket) I resist her sobbing because the tears represent her fatal flaw, that shameful lack of grit.

Clearly, Shana Feste deliberately engaged toughness (or lack thereof) as a theme, and I didn't like what she had to say about it one bit. And why not? What she said was likely honest. Sometimes people aren't tough; sometimes they can't muscle through. That's reality, and it *is* tragic. But like Lady Antebellum, Kelly is repulsive *because* of her authenticity. We don't want too much truth in our myth. The part of the myth that is so alluring is the untruth, the lie, the idea that anyone can be a Mattie, that weakness alone can bring Kelly down. (The film only distantly addresses her substance abuse, which is likely culpable for the bulk of her problems. Instead, we are told she is a mess simply because she isn't tough.) But what really gets my goat, if we're being honest, is that if one of these film's western women is the prototype, I much prefer the unlikely story of a gutsy fourteen-year-old blazing through Indian Territory to gun down a murderer than the much more common, truthful story of a woman battling and losing to an addiction. A woman as (seemingly) weak as Kelly has no attractive place in this story, and like the unseemly prostitutes and shut-ins, gall-less Kelly will be edited out. Our collective devotion to the dream of the tough-as-nails westerner prohibits us from abiding a tale as true as Kelly Canter's. Once we are engaged in the myth of the West, of hard soil and smoking six-shooters and leathery people with unreal ruggedness, we want to dream. We want to succumb to the romance and see Mattie racing Little Blackie through the frost-packed plains and imagine we could ride that fast, be that brave. We do not want the truth that sometimes grit isn't enough.

But I understand this susceptibility, problematic as it is. Because this is the thing about toughness: perhaps nothing else matters more to the western identity. All too often, one's worth is measured by the depth of her grit. Growing up, nothing was praised or appraised nearly as much as my ability to get up and push on. Most every westerner has moments of resolve they recall—perhaps only to themselves—with pride. When I was seven, my father and I camped deep in the Sawtooths, and I thought of that trip a lot as I watched Mattie ride with Rooster. At the core of Mattie's story is her father. Everything she does is for him. Her revenge is her mourning, and as I watch her, I wonder who taught her to ride and shoot. Who taught her to swallow down tears and keep going. I suspect we are both daughters who carry our fathers deep in our hearts.

We ditched the pickup at the trailhead and spent the week riding horses up basalt cliffs, across ledges of shale, to high mountain lakes cluttered with trout so wild they didn't know to fear our feet. Slick fins brushed anklebone. One afternoon, riding in a saddle with stirrups too long for my feet, I jumped a horse over a creek bed. When I went to lean into the stirrup, to brace myself for the landing, I slipped from the horse's back. My arm snapped. I lay in the dirt. My father jumped from his mare and picked me up. He wrapped my arm tight in his jacket. We rode the long way back to the truck. We were a day's drive from a hospital, and the road was gutted washboard. I lay in the back and braced against the jostle. Finally, I slept a deep, hard sleep.

For Christmas that year my father framed the X-ray of my arm, the glowing branch of my ulna cracked straight through. "My Right Hand Pistol," he'd scrawled across the bottom. For a decade that testament to toughness hung above my bed.

The body is its own attestation. Recall that fishhook sliced from my scalp. I remember my father squatting to show me the hook, red smeared and shining in the light. *Cut all the way to bone*, he'd said, and I could feel the blood sticking in my hair. I ran my fingers over the gash, stroking where the wound was already clotting, a scar already rippling, another kind of testimony.

If I took pride in my grittiness, then nothing was more shameful than my moments (and there were countless) of weakness. I think of all the situations I have winced at, the times when my stomach has flipped, my face paled, my eyes glassed with tears—the times I have been Kelly rather than Mattie. Here, the worst: My brother flew from a rope swing into the Payette River, a twenty-five-foot drop, a rope swing kids had died on. (The state cuts it down, but people keep tying it up. It is an Idahoan's rite of passage.) I got to the cliff's edge, took one hard pull, and then, just as my feet lifted, panicked. I tried to stop, but there was too much momentum. The rope flew away from me. The rapids went silent. The cicadas ceased. I only heard my brother yell my name. My arms groping for nothing, I fell and just missed the rocks.

My back scraped the sandbar, and when I came to the water's surface, my whole body shook. I never tried that swing again. Or another: Hiking with my parents, I nearly stepped on the paw of a sleeping cougar. My hands trembled, and I grew queasy. Or consider that ride out of the mountains with a busted arm, my medal of grit. What of it? Mattie's hardiness was so incredible because she didn't have to go with Rooster, didn't have to suffer through the "wild" lands, but she elected to. I was stuck in the woods with no option but to ride out, and I rode the whole way howling. I remember hitting the ground, the horse's hooves flying by me, and burying my head in the dirt, sobbing. All these moments when my toughness has waned, my grit (if it exists) lapsed, times that have felt like failings. I can't help but recall Mattie stony and strong as the snakes coiled around her, Mattie shooting down the bad man, Mattie riding out of that territory fevered from venom (and in the book, nursing a broken arm). Mattie cool as she maneuvered the business of her father's death. I can't help but feel weak in Mattie's long shadow.

Aren't these moments of lapsed grit reasonable, though? That a kid would panic at dropping from a cliff into a fast river? Or that knees would weaken in the proximity of a mountain lion? Or that a child would cry when a bone breaks? But we have no interest in our (perceived) failures. They're so commonplace and mundane. After all, we expect children to cry when injured or to tremble in the company of wild animals. What we don't expect are the rare (dreamed?) victories—the fishhooks and busted limbs. And maybe we want a myth to take stories of failure (aren't these "victories" really instances of stupidity—to stand behind someone casting a line or to jump a horse without my feet in the stirrups, dumb on both counts) and transform them into stories of triumph. Isn't this what a myth always does? Deserts turned to Bierstadt meadows; bland suburbs posing as frontier towns; broke Pa Ingalls transformed into a successful farmer. So too, my story of the busted arm was refashioned into a narrative of hard-core badassery, that X-ray nailed proudly above my bed.

Given my own rich history of wussing out, shouldn't I be able to see the ways in which Kelly and I are kindred spirits? Isn't my irritation unfair? But this thought occurs to me only weeks after I've watched the film. In the theater (Kelly collapsed in a bathroom stall, shaking with sobs), all I can think of is her husband saying she used to be tough as nails, and how sad he sounded, how bereft. And I bet this callousness traces back to my own western insistence on toughness, my own delusion that every woman must be a Mattie, that a Mattie can even exist.

For the third time I am unable to resist *True Grit*'s pull. On an otherwise uneventful Friday night, I buy tickets for Ryan and me, a large drink, and choose our seats carefully. (The woman in line ahead of us warned her son she didn't see how the Coens could top the Wayne classic. We sit away from her.) I cannot wait for him to see it, cannot wait to see it again. The lights die, and in the dark quiet, in that final moment when the screen crackles with PG-13 ratings and production logos, something has shifted. My Mattie crush has waned. Two weeks earlier, in a movieplex in Idaho, anticipating those opening lines about a girl avenging her father's blood, I'd been giddy, beside myself with expectations of popped triggers and flying bullets and Mattie's firm-jawed resolutions. But now I realize (as I did then but only halfheartedly) that Mattie is as realistic as Clark Kent, that I watch and rewatch her like a child poring through a comic book.

The lights die, and the music cues, and all that anticipation and fangirl glee have vanished. I've rejected lame, weak Kelly, but I can't buy into improbable Mattie. Understanding these unreal and unfair portrayals of female toughness, I am left a little irritated by both Shana Feste's cautionary tale of weakness and the Coen brothers' superhero of bravery. I realize Kelly and Mattie are both as flimsy and fantastic as the sweet-faced Ingalls clan, and I wonder if we have ever had the right kind of story, if there's ever been a western poster woman who rang true.

Usually, the myth fails me because it's outdated (roundups and wild horse herds) or too idyllic (homes overlooking fragrant mint fields) or too violent (outlaws and gunslingers) or too lame (Lady A's split, country pop identity), but here it fails me because this thread isn't even alluring. I look to it, and I am unconvinced. Maybe, then, my frustration has to do with knowing the reality too well. Clearly, this is a story I can't separate myself from (I am, after all, a western woman), and maybe I can't gain enough distance from my (untough) experiences to engage in this story. Maybe, for once, I'm tethered to the reality.

Whatever the reason, I'm unable to abide these far-fetched iterations, and isn't that what a myth is supposed to do? Enchant us? Transfix us? Allow us to imagine ourselves in its sharp light?

Maybe this is progress. Maybe here Kittredge would be pleased. Maybe he'd say we could all stand to look to the old model and feel a little dissatisfied. And maybe this is what I want for all of us—for the rodeo queens to accept that the West they promote is a dying one; for the ranchers to know their sons will probably become microchip manufacturers; for the cattle cutters to realize they are living in a limping legend. But more than anything, I want us all to know that after the illusions dissolve, somehow we press on.

The music begins, that sad piano prelude, and we pan through the night. Old Mattie narrates those opening lines, and something is missing. It's as though I'm watching a murder mystery knowing all the while that it was the husband's mistress. The fun has been spoiled, the dream wrecked. After all this reckoning, my enchantment, if it endures, is hollow. I have looked too hard for too long, and if I am to love this story at all, it is with the awareness that double-tough Mattie is only a fiction.

The Trouble with Two-Heartedness

> You just want to live in your
> own private Idaho.
> —The B-52s

Eagle is still ringed by a few farms—onion, alfalfa, maybe even mint. Corrugated rows flower with beet leaves or cornstalks. Dragonflies skim irrigation ditches, the fringes of farmland dense with crabgrass, bulrush, bluestem. For sale: forty acres.

My parents' ten acres is crowded. Their home, with its splintered porch and overgrown maple, dominates the hilltop. The barn, faded to the color of an old nail, squats to the north. A pond mucks the horse pasture. The garden spreads along the fence line. My sister's (still very new) home consumes the west end; even the sky is cramped—their horizon closed off by the Spanish tiled rooflines of Rio Bellisimo. But a few miles away, a hayfield for sale.

In thirty-five years my father's itch to claim has resurfaced, and this time it's even bigger: forty acres instead of ten, so he can build each of his kids a home. Forty, a number laden with biblical connotation. A whole people wandered forty years for a promised land, dreaming of milk and honey. Now my father dreams too. A bigger house for my sister and her ever-growing family. A one-story with a porch for Ryan and me. On the far end a spot for his only son. Room for a garden, a steer, a few colts. Across the lane farm fields; the deep smell of baled hay in August; of corn sweet on the breeze; of clotted, blooming lilac. Beyond the fields the foothills lit in dusky golds. The only homes in sight our own.

The first time I remember wearing cowboy boots, I was four years old. My father picked me up from preschool, and we drove to a cowboy supply store. I picked out black boots, black Wranglers, a red pearl-snap button-down, and a black cowboy hat. I ran my fingers along the felt brim, smelled the oiled leather, fiddled with the pearl snaps. This would be my uniform. While other kids played soccer or joined swim teams, I learned to barrel race.

My father saddled Misty, and I rode her in figure eights, dreaming of rodeos: the mutton busters clinging to sheep, the queens loitering in their halos of teased hair. The next night he set three barrels in a triangle. Uneasy at first, Misty sidestepped and snorted, but soon I nudged my heels into her flank, and we trotted. Each night she and I cut our way through the corral, and I went to bed smelling of dust and leather.

I mooned over horses, slept beneath a horse quilt, hung horse paintings on my walls, nailed Misty's thrown shoes above my bed. Most summers my father and I rode into the mountains, to the Bitterroots or White Clouds, and the last time I rode Misty I was thirteen. Deep into the Sawtooths we rode from dawn to dusk. I wasn't used to sitting saddle for such long stretches. Every muscle throbbed.

We dropped from a bluff. A grove of aspen shimmered in fading light. The woods thinned. The Sawtooths are chalk-gray mountains, jagged as their name implies, and nothing shy of knock-you-down pretty. A meadow rolled between white cliffs. A herd of elk sunned in the hollow, their antlers rising from wheatgrass. We stopped and watched as the elk shifted, as they lifted their racks to the waning light.

By the end of the trip, saddle sores blistered my thighs and calves. Back at the truck, too muscle-cramped to dismount, I slid from the saddle and fell to the ground. I was exhausted, dehydrated, probably a little sunstroked and generally, totally, untough. I went home, and my sores festered, but I was dazzled by those mountains, by their star-sparked skies and gray-white peaks, by the elk slow in the sun.

I understood then that I would always desire a place separate and my own. That I belonged in the open spaces. That a horse bowed to grass would always make my heart skip. I promised myself a home near the wild animals roving through light.

When I reapplied to college and landed in northern Idaho, I was charmed. The Palouse region is all hills deep in wheat. Moscow's tallest buildings are steel silos, and it felt like the West I'd seen in that *New York Times* ad. The mountains are small—hills really—and barely wooded. Stubbled and the color of a shallow lake, they are a different kind of beautiful. There I gave myself over to a particular kind of westernness.

Not surprisingly, it was in Moscow that I got the boots I wear now with such pride. I hadn't owned a pair since my barrel racing stint,[1] but for my twenty-fourth birthday Ryan bought me Frye boots—the same brand my father wore. They were the color of dandelion hearts, and I wore them every day.

The boots flipped a switch. I transformed from sheepish teenager—awkward in Boston—to proud Idahoan drinking whiskey in a Tucson bar. I bought the albums my parents had raised me on: Loretta Lynn, Waylon Jennings, Lyle Lovett. I sold my sedan and learned to drive Ryan's pickup. At dusk I sped through the wheat fields, arm out the window, hand open.

I felt like my parents must have thirty years earlier—like this place was Edenic and asking only to be taken.

Ryan and I imagined settling in a northern Idaho farm town, a place with more bars than grocery stores. I imagined a house like the one in the *New York Times* ad. A yellow kitchen with French doors and a long porch where we'd read and the dog would lap from its dish and when night fell we'd pull on sweaters and sit together until one of us said *Better go in* and the other would follow. I imagined pacing the meadow, saddling a quarter horse and riding her hard through hills and higher to ridges, the bluffs cast in new-day light. I imagined a place for us alone.

When I visited the Treasure Valley from Tucson, my romance dampened. I'd trailed rodeo queens and fallen behind. I'd tumbled from a lazy horse on a flat stretch of trail. I'd watched legit cowboys do their thing, and instead of blushing, I'd fantasized about a park bench and hot latte. If I felt out of step with rural Idaho, my time in the burbs hadn't been all bad. Eagle's Thai restaurant turns out a mean curry, and the farmers' market is chockablock with crepe stands and shining eggplant and monster-size peaches. On Sunday mornings I drank Bloody Marys in brick bistros. Too often I spent too much money on linen gauchos and organic cotton dresses in French-named boutiques. Women with severe haircuts slid silk tops into shining, embossed bags. I held the ribbon handles and walked to my car, a fresh spring in my step.

Now I think less about how this place has shaped me (hadn't my summer in the Treasure Valley answered that? I was someone who couldn't stay in the saddle but wore boots anyway, someone who lamented the bulldozed slaughterhouse but turned slowly—with relish and delight—in the boutique mirror. I was someone who reflected this place's halfhearted evolution). Instead, now I worry about finding a way forward.

Nearly a decade has passed since my father bought the alfalfa farm, and the land has brought trouble. My father, who runs that one-man legal practice in a converted farmhouse, bought the field from a client (only after appraising it, paying market value, and consulting an outside lawyer). When the client died before the deal closed, his distant cousin caught wind. He came like a claim jumper. He came in the tradition of *The Big Sky, Shane, Melvin and Howard.* He came for the promise of flipped land, easy money. No coincidence that the now-interested cousin is a big-name lawyer and land developer with high-up connections. He's said to build subdivisions like Rio Bellisimo—more mini-mansioned, themed communities. Though he had no direct claim to the land (he was not a trustee), he maneuvered a case against my father.

Initially, the case was quickly dismissed in my father's favor. But then the developer appealed and won. So my father appealed and won again, and then the developer appealed, and my father lost. When a verdict comes in, the opposing party appeals. So it has gone on for years.

Soon the case will go to trial again, but this time my father will be the defendant in a different way. At his last appeal the developer sued him for suing. Now my father fights for the right to keep fighting. The battle has become about more than the land (as these things so often do). It's about the pursuit of justice. In this way I hope my father wins.

"They're cagy bastards," I tell him.

"That's why you can't quit," he says.

I think of western films, stories about people fixed on fairness. I think of double-tough Mattie Ross and Rooster Cogburn, how they never pack it in, and I am inclined to cheer on my father. He hasn't got an ounce of quit in him. If I do not think about the broader implications of our possessiveness, then I see only my dad, hellbent on this dream for his family. I can think he's kind of a badass.

But I watch my father argue for another day in court, and I worry. I worry about my parents' finances; about their time and energy; about my father's inability to look at his ten acres, his granddaughter helping in the garden, his son-in-law mowing the lawn, and put those forty acres out of mind. I wish he could say he got a raw deal but those are the breaks and walk away. My father can't do this because he believes the white hats win. He believes in persevering. He believes in land worth fighting for. When my parents wed after those few weeks together, it was the myth—their shared dream of a pasture and a farmhouse and open prairie—that bound them. For them, too, it runs deep. And it's tough to quit a story that tells you to never quit.

With luck my father will win and he will build another home, a barn for his horses, a space for each of his kids. Or maybe he'll lose once and for all. Maybe another novelty neighborhood will crop up—a fake Dutch village littered with windmills or a subdivision dedicated to wine bottling or a hipster mini-Brooklyn. Just another thing pretending to be what it isn't.

My father and I are bound in our desire to claim. In Moscow I wanted my own farmhouse separate from town. When I click-clacked in my boots and sang at the Plant, I dreamed. There we were on the porch, drinking iced tea through the heat of the day. There we were in a kitchen with the windows open, cooled by a wind rich with wheat or pine. There we were driving down a dirt road to the highway with no stops between. However worried I had been about entitlement and conquest and mutual exclusivity mattered less. Maybe this was a result of my rural costuming. I had submitted to a story about what it means to be a westerner, and then, having played the part, I wanted to buy in.

People have always developed place, have always changed nature. All that remains is for us to consider the scale and impact of that change. It's my mother and the mint field on repeat. Her single home on ten acres doesn't affect the land the same way Richter's proposed forty-per-ten would have. And my father's four homes on forty acres would shape Eagle differently than another themed subdivision. My old farmhouse overlooking prairie wouldn't transform Moscow's landscape or culture in that fake Tuscan villa way. My father and I want large lots with room for a small crop and a few cows. Places that preserve rural character—at least a little, at least comparatively. We want to honor this place, not immediately transform it. I am inclined to say there is a right way to make a home here, and that way is my father's, mine.

But to an extent these are all variations on the same theme.

Homes on large lots invite fewer commuters and preserve at least some of the space they occupy. They strive for a kind of compromise, where domestic and wild might coexist. But they can also take a larger pull from water reserves. My parents' and sister's homes, for example, enjoy rolling, plush lawns. Beyond them the horse pastures are irrigated. Sprinklers chug through the hot summer months. Those big mansions on tiny plots have hardly a scrap of grass to tend. We all leave our mark.

And people have always come here for a million reasons. Some of us came for dawn tinting mountain lakes and some out of desperation or necessity. My parents reflect this: my father came for the postcard and my mother because it was the first out she got. Now droves move to Eagle desiring it just as it is. They delight in bonus rooms and tennis clubs and the affordable cost of living. They are thankful for Eagle's clean downtown with its white-latticed gazebo and haute cookie shop, for the polite neighbors and soccer leagues and water-spurting jungle gyms. They do not mourn its transformation because they prize livability over ruggedness. We all want different things.

In Moscow I wore boots and drove a pickup and sang about men who come home a-drinkin' with lovin' on the mind. I was smitten in that newcomer way, but maybe my affection was also shaped by my season in life. I was almost graduated from college and just married. Adulthood was *real*. Maybe I was lonesome for childhood. Maybe I conflated this place's past with my own.

My childhood can seem like a highlight reel of stereotypical westernness. A mare gleams with sweat. A deer breaks the glass of a high mountain lake. A father sets his daughter on a pony's back and hands her a gun. Saddle sores fester, and bones bust, and pistols smoke. But all that was short-lived. By the time I hit puberty, I seldom rode horses and would have sooner died than gone camping with my family. I wanted what most preteens want—to be sedated by MTV, to wander the mall in a pack of girls, all smelling of Clinique Happy and strawberry Lip Smacker. I wanted to sleep on trampolines and ride bikes in cul-de-sacs. I wanted to shriek at flat-abbed pop stars lip-synching live.

And it wasn't all country song lyrics. I didn't just barrel race. I played basketball and took acting classes and dreamed of a Boston brownstone as often as I imagined an unpeopled stretch of prairie. Each summer my parents sent us to Upstate New York to visit our grandparents. I saw Broadway shows and rode rollercoasters and dipped lobster in hot butter and ordered bagels with schmear. But the western parts were the parts I loved best.

When I returned from Boston, I resented my sister's home because the transformed pasture mirrored my own unwelcome transformation out of adolescence. In Tucson I sang Garth Brooks songs because they reminded me of being small enough for my father to buckle into his backseat and drive home. Back home I patted penned mustangs because I wanted to hunker down in a pickup bed and watch a blond stallion wait on a bluff, the wind caught in its mane.

If we are a people resistant to evolution, then here I am quintessentially western. Recall that rope swing above the Payette River. My brother grabbed it, arced above the water, and then, his body slack in the wind, dropped—a graceful parabola. I gripped the rope from that steep height. I pulled back and lunged but then, at the last moment, a stutter step. I was lucky I hit water when I fell, lucky to just have scraped my back. But it was the most *me* thing I could have done. I have only ever hesitated, have only ever dragged my feet. When evolving out of one season of life into another, I have held tight to the stabilizing rope of story.

I have ridden a horse into the Sawtooths just once since that last trip with Misty. I was twenty-two, and it was the week before my wedding. It was my father's idea. Him and his Right Hand Pistol, horses on a mountain trail, maybe even elk in a meadow. All that reiteration and sameness. I jumped at it.

I don't remember how far in we rode—if we stopped at a lake or a river or a bright, open meadow—but I know we were quiet.[2] In five days I would begin my own family. I was taking my final lunge into adulthood, and this was how we closed me out: sunburning in the saddle, ducking beneath branches, patting the mares' necks when they carried us high and far, eating bacon from a skillet and playing gin rummy on a log, just like we had all those many years ago.

In Moscow I was a newlywed on the cusp of college graduation. The future was a wide, black canyon I was scared to wander. I had found a man I loved, a town I loved, but sometimes I woke in the night. We lived in a studio apartment in a brick building nearly as old as the city itself. Outside our window, when the bars closed, sorority girls laughed and fell in the streets. Souped-up lowriders roared to red lights. Beside me Ryan rolled over, and the wrought iron groaned. I poured a glass of water and opened a window, and the air, damper this far north, settled thick in the lungs.

If I woke in my parents' home, I opened the window to the clear chill of a spring night, outside loud with bullfrogs and crickets and nothing else. Now the best parts of my past felt suddenly removed. When I pulled on boots and threw back whiskey, when I imagined a farmhouse at the end of a dirt lane, I grasped for the dreamed-of history of this place because it looked and felt so much like my own.

And what is that if not nostalgic and romantic? What is that if not stunted?

I was scared—in the way we all are, sometimes, I think—about what would come next. I was navigating change (again) and I got skittish (again). I defaulted to the comfort of the fantastic and familiar. And we should be leery of affection grounded in fear because there ain't a worse way to love a thing than that.

I have wanted conflicting things. I have longed for responsible development—regulating home-per-acre ratios, keeping housing centralized to already-existent downtowns, leaving the farm fields and foothills untouched—but then imagined a home overlooking the crest of a wheat field, chaff spangling in the light. I have hoped my father wins the hayfield, and I have wanted the field to remain crowded with hay and mint so the air changes with the seasons.

The hayfield will soon be swarmed by subdivisions, and those homes my father would like to build his kids will be another cycle of conquest, and my imagined home on the Palouse would be the next cycle after that. My father and I would both kill the thing we love.

Maybe my Moscow return wasn't such a sharp overcorrection. Maybe the pickup and boots weren't all prop and costume. There were a lot of reasons I had stepped back from the things that grew me, many of them practical. I got a boyfriend and a driver's license. I was a listless college kid, drifting from place to place. Now Ryan and I live in cheap apartments usually wedged between strip malls. The West my father showed me was one of privilege—to have the time and money and space to recreate.

But Ryan and I still seek nature's tonic as much as we can. In Tucson we backpack the Catalina Mountains, the Rincons, the Santa Ritas. We share an apple in the rare shade of a smoke tree. We sleep in our tent on creek shores. I am charmed in my usual way by saguaros that tower black in a sunset, by wrens that balance on their arms, by desert stars that burn white. And if we were in Idaho, we'd hike trails there too. I have never stopped connecting with landscape. The love, then, isn't all past tense. It isn't all prolonged adolescence. Some of it endures.

Now, though, my affection has morphed. I no longer turn to a defective story as an affront to change. Now I love but from a remove because I know the place I remember is gone. Or if it isn't gone yet, it's going fast.

The Palouse farmhouse wasn't the first home I imagined. When I was a child, there was a cattle field that stretched from the Boise River to a steep hillside. Aspen and willows shaded the shore. Sycamores and cottonwoods studded the flats. The field was a palm cupping light. *I'm gonna live there,* I'd tell my mother. Now the pasture is a neon-lit cineplex where you can wine-and-recline through Imax extravaganzas. I am the product of a place that is continually transforming and evaporating at breakneck speed. A place that is always under cultural siege. This calcifies the parts that were tender.

When people come here pursuing that wild place—the mustangs bucking through desert, the mountain trails fringed with suncups—I want to tell them, *Come, find them. They're here.* The elk still rove.[3] The sunsets are still fiery. But there are ugly parts too. Our entitlement and possession yield the worst kind of development. We get stuck in wars we refuse to quit. We haven't reconciled our conflicting ideas about what the West is or should be, have failed to live coherently. The transfixing parts remain but only in fractions. So love the epic, enchanting parts of this place—the most beguiling facets of the old story—but love them with a loose grip. Love them for what they are—remnants to behold because of their scarcity, not as a denial of it.

When Ryan and I dream our future, we still dream the same things. I still want to readily connect with wilderness. I still want to live separate from the suburbs. But I want to remember that when we claim a thing (regardless of our intentions, despite our degrees of impact), we change it. Five houses on a single acre or a single house on five acres. It all transforms.

When we picture that farmhouse, we quickly fill it with the children we hope to have. *There is so much we will show them,* we say. I imagine a child beyond the front porch, bending to lupine bunches. I see her peeling splinters from front steps. I see her asleep on my shoulder, smelling of lavender and sage. I see my father lifting her to a horse's back and leading her through a corral. I see Ryan teaching her to cast a fly line in a river bend, to keep the wrist straight, to read the water for calm eddies. I see us feeding her potatoes around a campfire. I see us leading her across wheatgrass meadows, down steep and dusty paths to the cool relief of a shallow creek. I see us pointing to a deer on a hillside, and watching her eyes follow.

I want to give her what I had. I want there to be something to give.

This Will See Us Through

Soon I'll finish graduate school, and I know, already, we won't stay put. Our time in the Sonoran Desert, living in a flat-roofed home the blushed-out color of a conch shell has been formative, lovely even. In the spring, which is to say February and March (when Moscow is still prone to snow), we sit on our back stoop in the thin shade of paloverde trees. Behind our house winds an unpaved path of beaten-down weeds and barrel cacti; it's a little haven from the rest of the city. Tucson is a big suburban tangle. Most streets, exempting a few funky sections near the University of Arizona's campus, are lined in run-down strip malls—sneaker outlets and fried food joints and a whole lot of gas stations. It reminds me of the Treasure Valley in this way. But if you press out into the desert, it's a color-leached, bony kind of beautiful. I hear if you stay here long enough, your eye learns to see the nuances in color, that this place can even look lush-ish.

But in late spring, when the heat closes over the city like a fiery mouth, or in autumn, when I know Idaho's fields will be stunned silver with the first freeze, I still imagine that Palouse house, its screen door slapping in a May breeze or its windows shining with hoarfrost—and it's charming as all get-out. Sure, we could make for that town and lock down that house, but we would be academics in a city of eight hundred people. As much as I love the harbored image (the lit porch at dusk, the prairie view at sunrise), I can't imagine how we'd build careers there, and I'd probably feel like a poseur or most definitely an outsider. Of course, we could go to Eagle, near my parents' ten acres, but this only seems like a theoretical option, one we know we'd never make good on. We're a little too unkempt for those square plots and matching homes.

Instead (with little discussion, as though it were inevitable), Ryan started looking for a camper shell and a new set of ThermaRests. Something about the simplicity of living from our truck won't be denied. And it's the sort of thing that made me fall in love with him—his desire to connect with place, his ability to live well with little. It is a small bucking of societal norms, of the tamed and boring trends I see in the Treasure Valley. It is a tiny rebellion played out, when I envision it, to the tune of "Me and Bobby McGee." It's a little ridiculous in this way (I realize).

We talk about parking it in a meadow in Stanley (a town of one hundred people on the bank of the Salmon River of No Return, near the base of the Sawtooth Mountains). It's one of the most beautiful spots in Idaho, in the near exact center of the state—the Salmon a sky-reflecting blue, the valley waving in knee-high wheatgrass, the Sawtooths looming white and ripping the sky. We'll cook from a campfire and hike in the morning and read by flashlight. We'll make like my parents thirty-five years ago, living from a car, sleeping in the grass, waking to neon skies.

This is what we tell ourselves at least. Certainly, we could do it; it all checks out: the pickup truck, the squattable meadow at the base of my favorite mountain range. And maybe we'll do it, and maybe it will be badass for the time that it takes. But when I imagine it, there's a pang of hesitation or guilt—quick but sharp. Our plan is so short-term. We can only live this way until we land jobs or our money runs out. And it risks yet another excursion into the belly of this myth. We'd wander the far corners of Idaho, skirting suburbia's reach, pretending we can go on like this forever, that the meadow is ours alone. We'd be clinging to a tooth-achingly sweet romanticism. Hawthorne said romance is nothing more than a "legend prolonging itself," and our pickup parked in the grass might seem a little prolonged, I know.

Richard Hugo wrote a poem about Philipsburg, Montana, titled "Degrees of Gray in Philipsburg." The poem goes something like this (as summarized stanza by stanza by Charles D'Ambrosio):

1. You're fucked
2. We're all fucked
3. Why?
4. Let's Eat Lunch

The poem is about a lot of things (descent, entropy, death, escape), and it describes one of those Old West towns that has been on the wrong side of boom-bust for ages (had Eagle been fifty miles from Boise instead of five, it would be, I imagine, a town like Philipsburg). Philipsburg is a place where only the church and the jail are kept up, where the few locals (the bartenders, jail keepers) are tired and raging. This town and its people are in a real sorry way. But you are just passing through, and in the poem's epiphanic moment, you remember that *the car that brought you here still runs.* In this I see despair and hope.

The car that brought you here still runs. I have encountered this line—a little bizarrely—four times in the last few weeks. First, I read it isolated from the rest of the poem, in (and this seems fitting) a Kittredge quote. In one of the final chapters of *Who Owns the West*, Kittredge offered this line as an example of our need to light out once in a while: "Our species, I think, is emotionally hardwired to every so often hit some road. Richard Hugo said, 'The car that brought you here still runs.' There come times, like midsummer, when we yearn for nights of dancing with strangers." I read this in our hot, little house—Ryan running guitar scales on the couch beside me, a fan blowing in oscillating drafts, a glass of ice water sweating by my feet—and I thought of our desire for the steep, switchback highways of central Idaho, for the view from a Stanley meadow.

Then a poet and friend of mine dropped the line in a social media post. I was scrolling in that mindless, late-night way, zipping past other people's photos of white beaches and charcuterie boards and plump babies, but then the line, then a halting. The poet has been Teaching for America in the Louisiana bayou, and next month he will pack up and return to the oil fields of Wyoming. "It'll be tough to leave that place," he wrote, speaking of the small town where he's worked with underprivileged first graders, "but the car that brought me here still runs." Here the line carries the same sentiment as Kittredge's but different: escape, but for another reason. The lucky can always leave, the poet suggested.

Most mornings, before the heat really means business, Ryan and I sit on the shaded patio of a café and drink cold coffee. We bring whatever books we are reading and are content in that liminal space between together and apart. We are quiet, save the sound of pages turning and ice chiming in a glass. Like this, the line found me again. Charles D'Ambrosio closed out his book *Orphans* with a whole essay devoted to the Hugo poem (which he included in its entirety), and for the first time I encountered the line in context, unexcerpted. I like the poem as much as I like that all-star, see-it-everywhere quote. Beneath the title—"Degrees of Gray in Philipsburg"—runs the opening line: "You might come here Sunday on a whim." An overcast western town, an impulsive passerby. Already I was all in. Philipsburg is a place like so many dots on the Idaho map—a town mostly boarded up and written about in the past tense. The poem's traveler pines for the romance of then ("the last good kiss you had was years ago"), and her car and life have broken down. Her rage turns eventually to boredom. I read this and remembered my return from Boston. My job at the Gap, the food court milkshakes, my aimless drives through just-built, poseur subdivisions. Frustration precursing malaise indeed. In the poem I see some of the saddest parts of the West. I see nostalgia and grief and loneliness and restlessness. I see different versions of myself.

I like D'Ambrosio's essay too. In it he describes Philipsburg as a place varnished in "nostalgia, where loss finds rest." He explains it is essential for the poet to ask questions (Hugo's third stanza is written exclusively in the interrogative), and he speaks to our tendency to stagnate: "The temptation, in art as well as life, is to fall back on old forms, to attempt an impossible repetition." D'Ambrosio makes a sharp case for poetry's power to descend, to relish those questions, to give us the power of language (where it too often fails), to illuminate our flaws, our rage, our nostalgia, and to get at the truth. Most important, though, D'Ambrosio says, "Poetry is the vehicle that broke down and brought Hugo here, to the degrees of gray, but it still runs, and the proof is the poem itself. The poem is what the poet brings back, that's his fortune." A deeper probing of the line than the "escape" interpretations, and it rang true. It's poetry (language? analysis? awareness?) that carries us forward.

In the poem's closing stanza, Hugo offers a beacon. The traveler orders lunch from a slender woman with hair so red it throws light like a flare. D'Ambrosio explains, "The light in the final line really refers to the act of seeing. It's about optics more than opportunity. The poem is the light." It's about lifting the bandana of delusion and disillusion. More than words on a page, maybe poetry is the thing that happens when we turn away from fruitless repetition and long-held misconception, when we cast ourselves headlong and slanted toward truth.

Hugo sees my frustration, boredom, and nostalgia. He speaks to my tendency toward stalling out and looking backward. More than that, though, he offers this: *Poetry is the car that still runs, and it will see us through.* Ryan refills my coffee and cracks a scone in half. I set down the book and eat the biscuit, satisfaction multiplied.

Finally, in the most recent and weirdest encounter, I found a picture of Ryan and me at a party we'd attended while I was studying at the University of Idaho. We are smiling politely, weirdly composed (we are on someone's porch, and people mill around us, most of them dancing; a haze of cigarette smoke fogs the scene), but to my left a guy stands on the photo's periphery, his presence an accident or afterthought. He has snuck into the background of our photo, and in a moment of drunken mischief, he lifts his shirt at the camera. He thrusts his hips out and sticks out his tongue. He yanks his tank top up to his shoulders. Magic Markered onto his belly, the one Hugo line.

Surely I've seen this picture before, which means, technically, that I've read the line before, but it didn't register then, and I didn't remember this kid or his homemade, fake tattoo. And how weird this all seems! That in the twenty-four hours, or however long it takes for marker to wash off, this particular line of poetry was scribbled on his chest, he and I would attend the same house party (countless of which occur every night in Moscow) and that he would be compelled to not only crash a near-stranger's photo but to, in a moment of *Girls Gone Wild*–like fervor, flash his chest, only to emerge years later, in my photo album, another instance of this line hunting me down. It's nearly celestial in its improbability.

Three weeks ago I'd never read the line; now, four times in two weeks. I try to keep away from superstition, but I've learned to revere repetition.

I have been content in the Southwest. Tucson is alive with its own rich identity, and for all of its sprawl, it remains distinct and textured. How gloriously it fuses cultures—Day of the Dead parades and taquerías and college kid head shops and New Age bookstores. But I visited Idaho and wondered (still!) about how this place shapes its people, how it's shaped me, how it's continually reshaping itself. The Treasure Valley is a land in transition. It's transmuting from a rural, sparsely populated state to an attractive, polished, New West mecca, and the transformation isn't all bad. *Forbes* regularly names Boise the number one place to raise a family, and it's the quickest-growing city in the nation. Now we enjoy more racial diversity, and the opera brings in bigger names, and Beard-nominated chefs curate seasonal menus. Museums and libraries are remodeled into shining fortresses. Folks in the Treasure Valley are fiercely proud of their spot in the world. They snowboard Bogus Basin in the winter, bike the foothills in the summer, buy hydrangea bouquets at the farmer's market year-round.

And I better understand the ways this place grew me, and I (mostly) like them. I'm no stranger to saddles and river rafts and snowboards. I appreciate how fleeting and lovely the pastoral can be—wheat bent in the breeze, horses blitzing a meadow. And I know that every place is ephemeral, always evolving, and there's no sense getting stuck in the grief of that.

I see the ugly ways in which I am inherently western too: my disproportionate, hypocritical insistence on toughness; my romance with things that are long dead; my unsustainable desire for a depopulated corner of Idaho; my own split suburban/rural identity. Though I've felt insufficient as a stereotypical Idahoan, I've had my (rare) moments of success—saddling a mare and running barrels, breaking camp while my father lay in the truck, his pelvis cracked. For all my griping about how boring and insufficient the burbs are (which I stand by), I must concede that I was a regular mall rat, working for my Gap discount, staying for blockbuster double features, scarfing cupcakes in riverside boutiques. So, for better or worse, I am fluent in two languages, prone to wander two different worlds.

Thirty years ago Kittredge said, "We are struggling to revise our dominant mythology." Today the struggle persists. The myth is too flawed, the reality too pale, and when tasked with choosing between the two, I've usually run full-bore to the haven of story. But ultimately, there's a dissatisfaction that edges out the intoxication, and it's bred from the place itself. The land is immune to myth. It tells the truest story there is, and the West's story is inherently an environmental one. We've got all that pride about place, that (emotional) attachment to the land. But in truth our entitlement has sparked environmental havoc. Consider Secret Waters, that fake town leapfrogging into the Boise hills. Like so many New West suburbs, it brought longer commutes, low walkability, low population density. It leaves a deep footprint. And it isn't just Secret Waters. The Treasure Valley is nearly nothing but ever-stretching subdivisions. Densely populated cities produce fewer carbon emissions per person than towns like Eagle. Its huge homes and the goods and services that accompany them guarantee higher greenhouse gases. The burbs are climate change's best friend, its steadfast enabler. And in the West our self-governing spirit jacks things up even more. Limited regulation allows developers to boom, boom, boom while only nominally mitigating their negative impact on local ecosystems and air and water quality. Nobody seems concerned about depleted water reserves, that classic western story. People here use more water than anyone on the planet (Americans use the most globally, and Arizonans, for example, consume nearly three times as many gallons per day as midwesterners). Just like those first white settlers who tilled a desert, we are faced with the same dilemma: From where will all the water come?

Our unchecked, rogue development echoes far and wide. Wildfires have always blazed through the West, but now they rage harder and longer. Higher temperatures, decreased snowpack, and longer warm seasons are all driving factors, and these factors are fueled, of course, by climate change, which is spurred by sloppy development. Globally, fire season has increased by 19 percent. In some regions wildfires consume four times more area than they did a decade ago. Idaho forests collapse. California cities turn to ash. The whole world burns hotter.

There are social implications at play too. Most Idahoans are peeved these days. Boise's growth pushes into all of the Treasure Valley, all of the state. Now, two hours into the desert, a hot spring–cum–spa offers cucumber sandwiches and mint water poolside. Just outside its entrance, cattle graze the prairie. Even those farm town holdouts like Nampa and Caldwell sit on shifting ground. Now Boiseans can take stretch Hummer limos to Caldwell's vineyards and ride back wine-drunk and grinding to Drake. This change means our delusional got-here-first "nativism" has reached a fever pitch. Idahoans are increasingly grumpy about their state's spiking popularity. All over town I saw T-shirts and ball caps with NO VACANCY stamped over the state's silhouette.

I understand this impulse. I have, as we know, been susceptible to mourning what's lost. To them with the sassy hat wear, I say *I get it*. But I also can't help but think we're mad at the wrong things. The problem can't be people. Everyone needs place. And if we follow this trajectory, we will be defined by our deficit in compassion, our shortfall in grace.

Instead of cultivating a spirit of antipathy, we might direct that frustration at the factors that drive people out of larger cities—the staggering cost of a home in San Francisco or Seattle, the crime rates that light fear in hearts, the crowded schools that shuffle kids through, the commutes that return parents home after children are asleep. All that income inequality and poor infrastructure. All those systemic failures. Instead of wearing snarky T-shirts or muttering about newcomers snatching up homes, maybe we'd be better served by making places—both those we escape and those we take harbor in—livable again. Maybe if we save the cities, we save the prairies.

My displeasure isn't confined to growth or shortsighted development. When I watched *True Grit* that final time, Mattie narrated the opening lines, and something seemed spoiled, her magic lost. She became lackluster, a shadow of her former self. On that last day in Idaho, I drove to the Marksman's, chose a .22, raised it fast and then, even faster, set it down. When I left Idaho, I landed in Tucson and desired only a long walk with my husband and nothing more. I did not—as I did in Boston—pine for some dream elsewhere. Now I think of my father's hayfield and wait eagerly for his day in court so all that battling can be behind us. Whatever had me smitten is nothing more than memory worth of elegy, and it's high time I take to reality.

Each time I've encountered the Hugo line, it's taken on new meaning. In Kittredge I see the glories of wanderlust, a vindication of my dream of living out of my pickup, scraping together enough money for cans of food and another tank of gas. I see (and this is likely me editorializing) an ode to romanticism. With the poet leaving his tough and heartbreaking work in Louisiana, I see not just our desire to escape but our need. Sometimes we hit the road because we can, and our mobility is a privilege. With D'Ambrosio I understand the line as an homage to the written word, as a testament to the power of language and sustained thinking. Here I see hope. And with the drunk boy in my photo, I am stumped. I don't know what compelled him to fling this line on his chest or what spurred him to flash my camera, but I take it to mean (in a turn admittedly romantic *and* superstitious) that this line is tracking me down, as though a poem can do such a thing, as though it can have such agency.

Like all good writing, the line embodies a myriad of meanings, and I believe each of them. But there's something else there too. For me it's about culpability. The line suggests I have just waltzed into Philipsburg, toured the dim-lit bars, the one church, the one jail, and now—having been charmed by its downtrodden-ness, having been spooked by its specters, having delighted in the ephemera of a vanished world—with an air of abandonment, I can leave. Or the more familiar story (maybe the one in which I'm most guilty): having been charmed and spooked and thrilled, I order my lunch, fall in love with the server with the red hair, and I stay—my running car a testament to my newcomer status. I am that wave of New Westerner who will squat here because the place itself is a vestige and I have been hooked on the romance that keeps me looking back.

Maybe this obsession points to my hunger for direction, and maybe it's made me a little mystical. But all superstition aside, I read the line and can't escape the duality of its message: Your car, oblivious tourist, is still running. You can finish your sandwich, tip the redhead, and move back to your booming town. Or: your car, dreaded newcomer, is warm-hooded in the parking lot because you've just rolled in, and even though you're unwelcome, you don't care because you refuse to grow up and move on (which is to say evolve) and you're determined to keep this legend alive.

But what I ultimately want to say is this: yes, it's weird that this line and I have collided, and its meaning (in all its manifestations) seems relevant to my relationship with Idaho, but more than anything, I am struck by my need to obsessively examine. I can't leave this line alone. After the fourth encounter, Ryan—equally rattled—suggested I tattoo it (and not with Magic Marker) on my hip. I can't shake the idea. I keep envisioning the one line, cursived across the bone, close by and awaiting yet another interrogation. I keep reading and rereading and analyzing, bouncing from Kittredge to D'Ambrosio to my own interpretation. I probe and sort; I oscillate between these two ideas that either I'm bad for leaving or bad for staying. I've been caught, trapped, loving a thing I know I'm better off leaving but loving it all the same. Regardless of which interpretation is true (meaning whichever Hugo meant? or whichever I find most apt?), all this fixating is nearly exhausting.

I've been just as obsessive in my considerations of Idaho and Idahoans. I sought out the vestiges—the ranchers and queens and mustangs. I sat in the bleachers and asked strangers to explain cattle roping and cutting. I felt embarrassed when they up-and-downed me and rolled their eyes, but I wanted to understand how they fit in a world that's largely left them and how I fit next to them. Now, with the Hugo line, I turn it in my mind like a stone slow to polish. Maybe this was all overkill or weird or excessive. Certainly, it was obsessive. And what good comes from unwearied examination?

I suspect a whole hell of a lot. For so long I was charmed by a particular vision of this place, but now I have looked too hard for too long. I know I can no longer envision my home as a land of mustangs running; cowboys cutting; queens waving; mothers plucking mint and fathers building homes and young girls running barrels, the corral dust-stirred from mares' hooves. All this obsessing cured me of that.

D'Ambrosio argued that poetry must ask questions so that it can invite "the salvational hopes of language, of poetry itself." Through this it strips away the delusions and gets to truth. It lifts the blindfold. It throws the light. Maybe obsession works in the same way. Maybe obsession, like poetry, drives us to look long and hard, to grapple our way out of our misconceptions. I read D'Ambrosio's essay in that light morning heat. Ryan's hand on my thigh, the scone buttery and warm, I felt grounded and directed. Communication saves us. Analysis and deep thinking and interrogation save us. Obsession saves us.[1]

If I could craft a new story for us to occupy, this is where I would start, with attention giving way to awareness, criticism, conversation. We need a model that teaches us to look closer and longer (at the place, the myth, ourselves) so that we become people who can sleep in a Stanley meadow knowing we're only passing through, that we are tenants at best, that the car that brought us here still runs.

I want a tradition that tells us to find our enchantment in reality, not in some epic long-gone dream. I want us to be soothed by the parts of the everyday that are as sanctified and sublime as the best parts of the myth: daughters in gardens, evenings on green-belts, brisk spring mornings and foamed lattes. I want to coun-terbalance that modern ethos by savoring and protecting the best, still-lingering parts of our past. I want a story that prizes the health of a place over our desire to claim it. A story populated by people who care *for* the land (not just about it) and prioritize sustainable, responsible growth. I want a story that says our strength lies in our ability to spot and resist the delusions of some Technicolor dream—the buckbrushed plains and lonesome heroes and mirages of unending land. I want a story that tells us we're tough enough to know when to call bullshit.

Tonight is a quiet Tucson night, save the winter birds warbling their songs, the lizards rattling the hopbush. Ryan grills salmon, I read on the back stoop, and soon we'll eat together on the steps, with the heat thinning and the sun setting. We'll go on like this for a while longer, pressing ice to our necks as the heat builds, point-ing to the sunset lighting up the whole alley, telling the other *Hot damn, that's a sight.* And then maybe we'll pack up and drive straight up this state, through the pink and dun desert to the rusted hills of Sedona, through the precariously rocked expanses of Utah, across the Idaho border. And maybe we'll remember that this place is always changing, and connected as ever, so are we.

Notes

Going West

1. I am referencing Idaho's tendency to be mistaken for Illinois or Iowa or a city in Oregon.
2. I say "imagined" here because obviously the land was settled by indigenous people with cultures as varied and distinct as Europe's—not only had they settled the land, but they'd developed it too. (Malcolm Margolin said Europeans found a Native American garden and returned it to a wilderness.) But the first white travelers saw this land, so sparsely populated compared to the places from which they'd come, as open, void.

   Of course, they also saw opportunity. From the beginning the American West has been about chance giving way to greed, possession, and violence. The crafted story about rivers running with gold, about people lighting out on a wing and a prayer, about families making a way on the plains, was a tool for westward expansion. And that white expansion led to the erasure of entire nations of indigenous people.

   Stories are multifunctional then. They fill voids, they make meaning, and sometimes they compel people to take what they want at genocidal cost.

Anywhere, USA

1. Interesting that most Idahoans (these days) were once Californians. The bulk of the 1990s newcomers came from the Golden State, which is to say they actually moved east. So here we see the myth eclipsing geography. The West has become a state of mind (which is, of course, just another way of saying it's a dream).
2. I take big issue with the use of the word *urban* here. Eagle is not a densely developed metropolitan center. Now it's a Boise suburb, though I concede that *suburb* does sound kind of derogatory; worth question-

ing why we don't call it "ex-rural" since *sub-* suggests inferiority, and it hasn't ever really had a relationship to the urban, but regardless of these failures of language, there's no way Eagle (or southwestern Idaho or Idaho at all) can be accurately called "increasingly urban"—not when all the growth is pushed out of the city center, not when the suburbs do the dominating.

Lady Antebellum

1. Naturally, he still wielded the privilege of a counselor of the law. If we got arrested for breaking curfew or were ticketed for drinking underage, my father showed up and swapped steep fines for preferred, clear-thinking classes. His work brought us other securities too. I didn't know many other people whose parents drove German cars or vacationed out of state.

2. Though I left the concert dissatisfied and Chris Harrison was leery of how well Lady A might deliver at the Grammys, it should be noted that the band took home the award for song of the year ("Need You Now"), best country album, best country performance, and best country song ("Need You Now" again). Taking home five Gramophones (a night high), the Lady cleaned up.

Ladies' Night

1. Of course, I am a little proud of my bangs and bruises. Recall how the rodeo queens rolled up their sleeves and showed off their scars. In this respect I am no different.

2. This is likely exaggerated in the proud mother sort of way. I don't remember anything from the rest of the day except feeling shocked when he stood and slapped the dust from his thighs.

True Grit, Country Song

1. Granted, I realize the Ingalls were real women, but it should be noted that the *Little House* books were overt propaganda, written as an idealized—and often utterly fabricated—portrait of independence and self-governing. Ingalls Wilder's daughter, Rose Wilder Lane, was, with Ayn Rand, a founding member of the Libertarian movement, and when Laura gave her daughter a manuscript about her life as a pioneer, Lane did some serious rewriting. She deleted most of their hardships, and the family became a clan of shining, libertarian heroes. Pa Ingalls, who

was in reality a failed farmer, became a successful self-run business-man, and his wife and daughters were his smiling supporters. The books were written in opposition to FDR's New Deal socialist ways, as a means of bolstering a political movement, so there is a great divide between the real Ingalls and the fabricated Ingalls characters. Like Bier-stadt's paintings, here I see another instance of this myth's cracked foundation, of just how much space swells between the reality and the story. Anyhow, onward.

2. A point of clarification: *True Grit* grossed $250 million nationally, while *Country Strong* pulled down a paltry $20 million. Perhaps the anoma-lous crowd trends say something about Arizona's taste for sugary sob stories or its insistence on bucking societal norms, or maybe both. I can't be sure.

Trouble with Two-Heartedness

1. Those boots were hardly worn. My rodeo career didn't last long. I showed up to my first race and, after eyeing the farm kids who'd trucked in for the meet, kids who wore spurs and flew around those barrels so fast they bounced out of their saddle with each gallop, I skipped out. My friend and I rode our horses into downtown Eagle and bought sodas and Cry Babies at the 7-Eleven and decided get-ting sugar-sick in the saddle was way better than racing with all those people watching. That seemed terrifying, and I never went back.

2. I do remember, though, the fear I'd felt. The trail cut along cliffs the color of mountain lions, and I never stopped sweeping for cougars. After we made our way back to the trailer, we led the horses down a hill to drink from a creek. We walked them, tired old mares, giving them a break. But the whole way down, I looked behind me, making sure the horse's hoof wouldn't clip my heel. Then, when it was time to trailer up, my heart raced when I squeezed beside the hindquarters. These were things I'd been raised to consider, to check for and then move on. But now I just plumb feared them. I never relaxed. Just add that entire trip to the montage of my prolific pansy-assing.

3. Sort of. The *Guardian* reported that a trail outside of Vail, Colorado, has become so trafficked—with mountain bicyclists and backcountry skiers and hikers and motocrossers—that the roughly one thousand elk that live in that region have dwindled to fifty-three.

This Will See Us Through

1. D'Ambrosio said: "Down is the direction poetry travels on the page . . . Down is where the poetry is." I see a confluence here between spatiality and obsession too. On the physical page, I am unwilling to leave a single thread intact, unwilling to mind the tight borders of a main text. Instead, I spill over. I press past the hard stop of a chapter's end. I branch out and digress and exist in layers of concession and doubt and mental doubling back. I obsess, and that obsession pushes out and plumbs low so that it can eventually, hopefully, lift back up.

In the American Lives Series

To order or obtain more information on these or other University of Nebraska Press titles, visit nebraskapress.unl.edu.

CPSIA information can be obtained
at www.ICGtesting.com
Printed in the USA
LVHW091400280720
661742LV00002B/472

9 781496 220219